WORLD HISTORY SERIES ■ ■ ■

The Spread
of Islam

Titles in the World History Series

The Age of Feudalism
The Age of Pericles
The American Frontier
The American Revolution
Ancient Greece
The Ancient Near East
Architecture
Aztec Civilization
Caesar's Conquest of Gaul
The Crusades
The Cuban Revolution
The Early Middle Ages
Egypt of the Pharaohs
Elizabethan England
The End of the Cold War
The French and Indian War
The French Revolution
The Glorious Revolution
The Great Depression
Greek and Roman Theater
Hitler's Reich

The Hundred Years' War
The Inquisition
The Italian Renaissance
The Late Middle Ages
The Lewis and Clark
   Expedition
Modern Japan
The Punic Wars
The Reformation
The Relocation of the
   North American Indian
The Roman Empire
The Roman Republic
The Russian Revolution
The Scientific Revolution
The Spread of Islam
Traditional Africa
Traditional Japan
The Travels of Marco Polo
The Wars of the Roses
Women's Suffrage

The Spread
of Islam

by
John Dunn

Lucent Books, P.O. Box 289011, San Diego, CA 92198-9011

Acknowledgment

*The author wishes to thank Gene R. Thursby, professor of religion
at the University of Florida, who provided useful and insightful
commentary on the manuscript.*

Library of Congress Cataloging-in-Publication Data

Dunn, John, 1949–
    The spread of Islam / by John Dunn.
        p.   cm.—(World history series)
    Includes bibliographical references (p.   ) and index.
    Summary: Traces the origins, spread, development, and
modern practices of Islam.
    ISBN 1-56006–285–1 (alk. paper)
    1. Islamic Empire—History.   2. Middle East—History—
1517– 3. Africa, North—History—1517–1882.   [1. Islamic
Empire—History. 2. Islam.]   I. Title. II. Series.
    DS38.3.D86   1996
    909'.097671—dc20   95-51795
                                                       CIP
                                                        AC

Contents

95409

Foreword

Each year on the first day of school, nearly every history teacher faces the task of explaining why his or her students should study history. One logical answer to this question is that exploring what happened in our past explains how the things we often take for granted—our customs, ideas, and institutions—came to be. As statesman and historian Winston Churchill put it, "Every nation or group of nations has its own tale to tell. Knowledge of the trials and struggles is necessary to all who would comprehend the problems, perils, challenges, and opportunities which confront us today." Thus, a study of history puts modern ideas and institutions in perspective. For example, though the founders of the United States were talented and creative thinkers, they clearly did not invent the concept of democracy. Instead, they adapted some democratic ideas that had originated in ancient Greece and with which the Romans, the British, and others had experimented. An exploration of these cultures, then, reveals their very real connection to us through institutions that continue to shape our daily lives.

Another reason often given for studying history is the idea that lessons exist in the past from which contemporary societies can benefit and learn. This idea, although controversial, has always been an intriguing one for historians. Those that agree that society can benefit from the past often quote philosopher George Santayana's famous statement, "Those who cannot remember the past are condemned to repeat it." Historians who ascribe to Santayana's philosophy believe that, for example, studying the events that led up to the major world wars or other significant historical events would allow society to chart a different and more favorable course in the future.

Just as difficult as convincing students to realize the importance of studying history is the search for useful and interesting supplementary materials that present historical events in a context that can be easily understood. The volumes in Lucent Books' World History Series attempt to present a broad, balanced, and penetrating view of the march of history. Ancient Egypt's important wars and rulers, for example, are presented against the rich and colorful backdrop of Egyptian religious, social, and cultural developments. The series engages the reader by enhancing historical events with these cultural contexts. For example, in *Ancient Greece*, the text covers the role of women in that society. Slavery is discussed in *The Roman Empire*, as well as how slaves earned their freedom. The numerous and varied aspects of everyday life in these and other societies are explored in each volume of the series. Additionally, the series covers the major political, cultural, and philosophical ideas as the torch of civilization is passed from ancient Mesopotamia and Egypt, through Greece, Rome, Medieval Europe, and other world cultures, to the modern day.

The material in the series is formatted in a thorough, precise, and organized manner. Each volume offers the reader a comprehensive and clearly written overview of an important historical event or period. The topic under discussion is placed in a broad historical context. For example, *The Italian Renaissance* begins with a discussion of the High Middle Ages and the loss of central control that allowed certain Italian cities to develop artistically. The book ends by looking forward to the Reformation and interpreting the societal changes that grew out of the Renaissance. Thus, students are not only involved in an historical era, but also enveloped by the events leading up to that era and the events following it.

One important and unique feature in the World History Series is the primary and secondary source quotations that richly supplement each volume. These quotes are useful in a number of ways. First, they allow students access to sources they would not normally be exposed to because of the difficulty and obscurity of the original source. The quotations range from interesting anecdotes to far-sighted cultural perspectives and are drawn from historical witnesses both past and present. Second, the quotes demonstrate how and where historians themselves derive their information on the past as they strive to reach a consensus on historical events. Lastly, all of the quotes are footnoted, familiarizing students with the citation process and allowing them to verify quotes and/or look up the original source if the quote piques their interest.

Finally, the books in the World History Series provide a detailed launching point for further research. Each book contains a bibliography specifically geared toward student research. A second, annotated bibliography introduces students to all the sources the author consulted when compiling the book. A chronology of important dates gives students an overview, at a glance, of the topic covered. Where applicable, a glossary of terms is included.

In short, the series is designed not only to acquaint readers with the basics of history, but also to make them aware that their lives are a part of an ongoing human saga. Perhaps they will then come to the same realization as famed historian Arnold Toynbee. In his monumental work, *A Study of History*, he wrote about becoming aware of history flowing through him in a mighty current and of his own life "welling like a wave in the flow of this vast tide."

Important Dates in the History of Islam

A.D.	570	600	650	700	750	800	850	900	950	1000	1050	1100	1150	1200	1250	13

A.D.

570
Muhammad is born.

595
Muhammad marries Khadījah.

610
Muhammad has visions in a cave.

613
Muhammad begins to preach in Mecca.

622
The Hegira begins.

624
Muslims defeat Meccans at Badr.

630
Mecca becomes the spiritual capital of Islam

632
Muhammad dies; Abū Bakr becomes first caliph.

634
Abū Bakr dies; 'Umar becomes caliph.

637–641
Muslims conquer Jerusalem, Persia, and Egypt.

644
'Umar is assassinated; 'Uthmān becomes caliph.

656
'Uthmān is assassinated; 'Alī becomes caliph and fights at Battle of the Camel.

657
Mu'āwiyah's forces challenge 'Alī.

661
'Alī is killed by a Kharijjite; Mu'āwiyah becomes caliph and moves capital to Damascus.

680
Yazīd succeeds Mu'āwiyah; Husayn is killed.

691–694
Dome of the Rock is erected in Jerusalem.

732
Charles Martel's forces hold back Muslims near Tours.

747–754
Abbasids overthrow Umayyad rule.

764
Baghdad becomes new Islamic capital.

786
Hārūn ar-Rashīd becomes caliph.

827
Mu'tazilite teachings become official doctrine.

833
Al-Mu'tasim becomes caliph and surrounds himself with Turkish guards.

910
Fatimads take control of North Africa.

969
Fatimads seize Egypt.

998
Mahmūd of Ghazni penetrates northwest India.

1055
Seljuks capture Baghdad.

1061
Spanish Christians begin Reconquista against Muslims.

1071
Seljuks conquer Asia Minor.

1099
Crusaders attack Jerusalem.

1147–1149
Europeans launch Second Crusade.

1187
Saladin recovers Jerusalem for Muslims.

1189–1192
Third Crusade takes place.

1202
Fourth Crusade.

1211
Turkish Muslims create Delhi sultanate.

1221
Mongols destroy Persia.

1258
Mongols destroy Abbasid power in Baghdad.

1260
Mamluks defeat Mongols.

1300
Crusades end.

1379
Tamerlane invades Persia.

1398
Tamerlane invades India.

1453
Ottomans conquer Constantinople.

1492
Last Muslim stronghold in Spain falls to Christians.

1500
Muslim Turks set up sultanates in northwest India.

1501
Safavids take control of Persia.

1520
Süleyman the Magnificent takes power.

1527
Ottoman troops are stopped at Vienna.

1556
Akbar becomes emperor of India.

1586
Shāh ʿAbbās controls Persia.

1627
Shāh Jahān assumes power in India.

1658
Aurangzeb becomes emperor; fails to conquer all India.

1683
Ottomans are defeated at Vienna.

1798
French troops land in Egypt.

1803
British occupy Delhi.

1805
Muhammad ʿAlī Pasha takes control of Egypt.

1808
Janissary Corps assassinates Selim III.

1826
Mahmud II begins reform of Ottoman Empire.

1853
Crimean War begins.

1908
Young Turks revolt begins.

1912–1913
Balkan Wars; Ottomans lose territories.

1914–1918
World War I; Ottoman Empire is destroyed.

1916
Arab revolt against Ottomans begins.

1918
Great Britain agrees to Zionist demands.

1922
Atatürk weakens Islam's hold on Turkey; Reza Khan begins modernization reforms in Iran.

1930–1950
Nationalism movement in Muslim lands.

1934
Ibn Saʿūd takes over Arabia.

1947
Partition of India and Pakistan begins.

1948
Israel founded; Arab League formed in response.

1967
Israel defeats Arabs in Six-Day War.

1979
Muslim fundamentalist revolution succeeds in Iran.

1980–1988
Iran-Iraq War.

1991
Persian Gulf War begins.

Allahu Akbar!

Allahu akbar! (God is most great!) Rich with multiple layers of spiritual meaning, these two simple Arabic words dramatically changed the course of history. They also formed the very core of today's fastest growing religion on earth: Islam.

Like Judaism and Christianity, Islam emerged in the Middle East, the youngest of the three great faiths. Its creed is simple and clear: there is only one God, or Allah; and the last in a long line of prophets chosen to reveal God's truths was Muhammad, a simple Arab merchant who rose from obscurity to greatness.

Islam offers its followers, who are called Muslims, a core of religious beliefs, a system of right and wrong, and a code of behavior to live by. The rules and commandments that make up what is known as the Straight Path appear in the Quran, or Koran, Islam's holiest book, which Muslims believe was transmitted from God to the prophet Muhammad.

But over the centuries since Muhammad's first visions from Allah, Islam developed into something more than a major world religion. It also became a powerful legal, governmental, social, economic, and cultural force that unified hundreds of millions of people dwelling in many far-flung lands. Spread by both word and sword, Islam swiftly unfolded as the basis for a vast, complex, and mighty empire that spread from the Atlantic coast of North Africa to China and India. No other realm has ever encompassed a greater mixture of diverse ethnic, racial, and linguistic types than Islam. Even Rome at its pinnacle paled in comparison to the range of Muslim authority. Writes historian William McNeill:

> Never before or since has a prophet won such success so quickly; nor has the work of a single man so rapidly and radically transformed the course of world history. Through his inspired utterances, his personal example and the organizational framework he established for Islam, Muhammad laid the basis for a distinctive new style of life which within the space of two centuries attracted the allegiance of a major fraction of the human race.[1]

Today almost a billion humans claim to be Muslims. Such a vast number is an increase from when Islam's very first believer was a modest merchant meditating in the darkness of a cave in a vast and barren desert.

1 The Origins of Islam

Islam came to life during the seventh century A.D. in the Arabian Peninsula, the largest peninsula in the world. Located in the Middle East, it is bounded by the Red Sea, the Arabian Sea, the Gulf of Oman, and the Persian Gulf. This huge but thinly populated land had a string of small seacoast market towns where people lived and worked as traders and artisans. And it had patches of farmlands where Arabs tried to raise crops of grain and orchards of dates, figs, and lemons.

But Arabia was mostly an arid, hot territory with an interior landscape of shifting sands and lethal heat. Three-fourths of the area's middle eastern land, in fact, is desert. Scattered oases of palm trees and water sources, which can only be tapped with deep wells, dot the middle stretches of the peninsula. The air is often thick with suffocating windblown sand. In the past desert-dwelling Arabians needed long robes and headgear for protection against the merciless sun, which blisters the skin and dehydrates the body. At night, though, temperatures drop to near freezing.

The Arabian Desert was, and still is, a world where a lone individual could quickly perish. Only by living and cooperating with others could anyone hope to stay alive. No people ever mastered such desert survival better than the Bedouin, nomadic desert Arabs who followed their flocks of goats across the burning wastelands from one isolated pasture to the next. The camel, their chief animal of transportation, provided much to their way of life. Bedouins drank camel milk and used the animal's dung for fuel, meat for food, and hide and hair for clothing and tent material.

Tribal Loyalty

Before Muhammad, Arabia was a country in name only. Most Arabs gave their loyalty to their tribe, not a nation, state or religion. Because life was hard and often short in the desert, these nomadic people lived by a stern code of *asabiyya*, or clan spirit, which was based on tribal unity, loyalty, and swift revenge. Observes author Huston Smith: "The Bedouin felt almost no obligation to anyone outside his tribe. Scarcity of material goods and a fighting mood chronically inflamed by the blazing sun had made brigandage [living by plunder] a regional institution and the proof of virility [manhood]."[2] As such, blood feuds, in which a tribe would kill someone in a murderer's family and result in a cycle of revenge between tribes, were common on the Arabian Peninsula.

Illiterate, superstitious, and warlike, the Bedouin were also a rugged, proud, and defiant people. Although they could be courteous and generous, they were also capable of great cunning and hardness. In pre-Islamic Arabia, for example, a man might kill an unwanted infant or rob a wayward family lost in the desert.

Ancient Religious Beliefs

Before the arrival of Islam, most Arabs worshiped many gods. They found deities in the sun, the moon, and in the desert winds and mischievous and evil spirits, or jinn, which frequented the natural world everywhere. Writes historian Will Durant in *The Age of Faith*:

> [The Arab] seems to have given scant thought to a life after death; sometimes, however, he had his camel tied foodless to his grave, so that it might soon follow him to the other world,

and save him from the social disgrace of going on foot in paradise. Now and then he offered human sacrifices; and here and there he worshiped sacred stones. [3]

The most important of these holy stones was found in a trading village called Mecca, which lay fifty miles from the Red Sea coast. Pilgrims traveled here from faraway places to see the Kaaba, an ancient, mysterious, cube-shaped shrine revered by Arabs for centuries. Imbedded in the Kaaba was a black stone, most likely a meteorite, which gave the shrine an aura of mystery. By the sixth century A.D. Mecca had become a major holy site for religious pilgrimage, thanks to the presence of the Kaaba, which most Arabs believed was home for some 365 gods. The most important of them all was al-Lah, whom the Meccans called the creator of the universe.

Arid, hot, and rocky Mecca, however, was hardly a desirable place to live. Perhaps its real importance came from its lo-

The Arabian Desert is a hot, inhospitable place where a lone individual has little chance of staying alive. In pre-Islamic Arabia, the nomadic Bedouins mastered desert survival by living cooperatively.

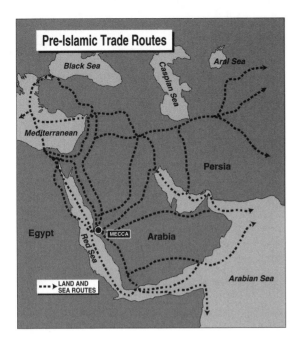

Pre-Islamic Trade Routes

Black Sea

Aral Sea

Caspian Sea

Mediterranean

Persia

Egypt

MECCA

Red Sea

Arabia

Arabian Sea

LAND AND
SEA ROUTES

of Mecca and the Kaaba. They assumed the responsibility and authority for guarding the shrine, collecting all tributes, and running the government of Mecca.

Little did anyone realize, however, that during the year A.D. 570 a certain baby boy was born in Mecca who would one day smash the power of the Quraysh and also launch an empire.

His name was Muhammad.

A Prophet Is Born

"Though we have abundant testimony about Muhammad's earthly life, most of our knowledge of him comes from second or third hand; the earliest surviving biography was written nearly a hundred and fifty years after his death," writes Robert Payne in *The History of Islam.*[4] Nonetheless, scholars have pieced together a compelling account of his extraordinary life.

Muhammad was orphaned at the age of six when his mother died. His father had died on a business trip two months before Muhammad was born. As a result Muhammad was reared first by a grandfather and then an uncle. Like most of the other three thousand Meccans, the boy received little formal education and may never have learned to read or write in his native tongue, Arabic. He was a stocky, dark-eyed, broad-shouldered youth with rosy-white cheeks whose hard work earned him the nickname the Trustworthy. Muhammad was also quiet, reserved, and unusually thoughtful about the spiritual side of life for someone his age. An early account of Muhammad states that when he was twelve years old, a Christian hermit in the Syrian Desert predicted greatness in

cation. Situated midway along the west coast of Arabia and only forty-eight miles from the Red Sea, it was also a favorite stopping place for wandering travelers who arrived in caravans of camels. The caravans, sometimes containing as many as four thousand camels, carried spices, precious metals, silk, ivory, and many other goods and foods. Sometimes these ships of the desert stretched more than a mile long. The constant arrival of so many Arab traders and merchants to Mecca and the Kaaba created a thriving merchant class.

Mecca's most powerful family was the Quraysh, which ruled the city. Even their religious preference governed business. The Quraysh believed that al-Lah, or Allah, was superior to all other gods. Meccans were required to offer tribute to Allah by paying a tenth of their crops and the first-born of their flocks. This wealth was collected by priests appointed by the Quraysh family, who believed they were the descendants of the ancient founders

Muhammad rose from humble beginnings to become one of the world's most powerful religious figures.

Arabian polytheism and who, like Christians and Jews, believed in just one God.

Muhammad surely must have also learned that Christians and Jews stressed the importance of a messiah, a savior sent by God to spiritually uplift believers. Christians believed that their savior, Jesus Christ, had already come. Jews, meanwhile, still awaited the messiah's arrival.

Christians and Jews had something else in common: their own holy books, which they believed were divinely inspired and offered spiritual guidance and deliverance.

"An Acute Sense of Inferiority"

In contrast, many Arabs of the time compared themselves unfavorably with Jews and Christians because they lacked a holy scripture and expectations of a savior. Writes Karen Armstrong in *Muhammad: A Biography of the Prophet*:

> Some of the Arabs believed that al-Lah whose name simply meant the God, was the deity who was also worshiped by the Jews and the Christians. But unlike the "people of the scriptures" as the Arabs called these two venerable faiths, the Arabs were painfully aware that He had never sent them a revelation or a scripture of their own, even though they had His shrine in their midst from time immemorial. Those Arabs who came into contact with the Jews and Christians felt an acute sense of inferiority; it seemed as though God had left the Arabs out of His divine plan.[5]

Over time tension developed between Arabs and Jews. One Arab recalled of these

the boy, claiming he would one day become a prophet.

During his childhood and adolescence Muhammad worked both as a sheepherder and a merchant. Later, as a young man, he went to work for a caravan business run by Khadījah, a warm-hearted, attractive widow who was fifteen years his senior. As her employee, Muhammad often traveled in a caravan on business trips as far north as Syria. During these journeys he encountered new religious beliefs such as those held by Christians, Jews, and *hanifs*—hermits who were unhappy with early days in Muhammad ibn Ishāq's *The Life of Muhammad*, perhaps the original biography of the Prophet:

> We were polytheists worshipping idols, while they [the Jews] were people of the scriptures with knowledge which we did not possess. There was continual enmity between us, and when we got the better of them and excited their hate, they said: "The time of a prophet who is to be sent has now come. We will kill you with his aid. . . . " We often used to hear them say this.[6]

Muhammad Settles Down

One day, at the age of twenty-five, Muhammad received a note from his employer that dramatically changed his life: "O son of my uncle, I like you because we are relations, and also for your good reputation among the people, your . . . good character and truthfulness."[7] Khadījah ended the note with a proposal of marriage.

The young man gladly accepted the offer. He had little reason to regret his decision. Within a few years his marriage brought him wealth, several children, and financial security. He also became a respected and well-known man of Mecca. Desmond Stewart provides this description of him in *Early Islam*:

> Despite his temperate nature, he is said to have had a forceful personality, and he must have made a striking appearance: handsome and burly, with massive shoulders, large hands and feet and a wide forehead above dark, bushy eyebrows and deep, large black eyes. He was of medium height and

walked with his head, which was unusually large, thrust impetuously forward. When spoken to he turned not only his head but his whole frame to face the speaker. When he was angry, a conspicuous vein swelled between his brows.[8]

Muhammad lived happily with his family for several uneventful years. Suddenly in 610, his fortieth year, something happened to him that not only transformed his life but also changed the world.

Visions in a Cave

During the holy month of Ramadan, roughly equivalent to September, Muhammad visited Mount Hira, located not far from Mecca. Here he liked to spend his evenings meditating and praying in an isolated cave. One night while he was alone meditating in this hideaway, he heard a strange tinkling of bells. Then a voice spoke to him in the darkness and commanded him to read. Terrified, Muhammad replied that he could not read. The mighty voice thundered: "Read!"

When Muhammad asked what he should read, the voice blasted:

> Read in the name of your Lord, the Creator,
> Who created man from a clot of blood!
> Read! Your Lord is most merciful,
> For he has taught men by the pen
> And revealed the mysteries to them![9]

Next, according to Muhammad, a silk scroll with a flaming script appeared before him. For the first time in his life, he

This miniature from the Royal Asiatic Society shows the angel Gabriel hovering above Muhammad (on horseback).

managed to read. Petrified with fright, he then went outside. What had happened to him, he wondered. Was he possessed by demons? He was so upset that he considered throwing himself off a cliff. All at once a voice boomed down from heaven. It was, says Muhammad, the voice of the angel Gabriel. Suddenly Muhammad turned his gaze skyward and witnessed an angel shining brilliantly above him. A moment later it disappeared.

Profoundly shaken, Muhammad fled to the arms of his wife and told her what had happened. As Khadījah listened, she overcame any doubts and believed him fully. Next she took her husband's story to a holy man, who declared that Muhammad had been approached by the same spiritual force that had once visited Moses, the great leader of the Jews.

Muhammad was now convinced that Allah indeed had chosen him for a special mission. But what should he do next? He waited for further revelations. After several days passed without further word from God, Muhammad returned to Mount Hira, hoping to duplicate his first encounter. Still nothing happened.

Two long years passed as Muhammad continued to wait in vain for further revelations. During this time, say some historians, he became dangerously despondent. Just when his spirit sank so low that he again considered suicide, we are told, Allah at last communicated to Muhammad again. These visitations, however, took a toll on him. Sweat broke out on his body. Sometimes he would faint, fall to the ground, and go into convulsions. His hair is said to have turned gray.

But the revelations made more than a physical impact on Muhammad. He also felt spiritually transformed. He received Allah's clear commandments. He now understood his mission. He was a prophet of God. It was time to act.

Muhammad Begins to Preach

In 613 Muhammad began to preach a new faith on the streets of Mecca. In the future Islam would develop into a complex and richly textured religion with many doctrines, rituals, and traditions. But during these early days Muhammad's message was simple and direct. He was, he proclaimed, a prophet of the one, true God, Allah, who created and ruled the universe. All must thank and worship Allah. The rich were commanded to share with the poor. Believers, said the Prophet, were equal before Allah. He warned that a day of judgment was coming when Allah would determine what kind of afterlife each person was to have.

Initially Muhammad seemed to believe that his faith was an extension of the monotheistic, or single god, beliefs of the Christians and Jews. He fully expected these groups to consider him the latest in a long series of prophets. When this failed to happen, Muhammad was greatly disappointed.

Nor were many Kaaba worshipping Arabs interested in the ideas of a forty-year-old merchant turned preacher. At best, the powerful Quraysh family tolerated him. Some members of the tribe thought Muhammad was acting foolishly and refused to take him too seriously. After all, the town brimmed with believers of many faiths and gods. What was one more voice?

Nonetheless, a few Meccans did embrace Muhammad's new faith. The first to become a Muslim, or follower of Islam, was Khadījah. The next three to join him were Muhammad's cousin 'Alī, a servant

An Angel in the Cave

Muhammad's main biographer, Muhammad ibn Ishāq, relied on Muslim tradition to produce this alleged account of the Prophet's encounter with the angel Gabriel. This excerpted version comes from Will Durant's The Age of Faith.

"Whilst I was asleep, with a coverlet of silk brocade whereon was some writing, the angel Gabriel appeared to me and said, 'Read!' I said 'I do not read.' He pressed me with the coverlets so tightly that me thought 'twas death. Then he let me go, and said, 'Read!'. . . So I read aloud, and he departed from me at last. And I awoke from my sleep, and it was as though these words were written on my heart. I went forth until, when I was midway on the mountain, I heard a voice from heaven saying, 'O Mohammed [Muhammad]! thou art the messenger of Allah and I am Gabriel.' I raised my head toward heaven to see, and lo, Gabriel in the form of a man, with feet set evenly on the rim of the sky, saying, 'O Mohammed! thou art the messenger of Allah, and I am Gabriel.'"

named Zaid whom Muhammad had freed from slavery, and a relative named Abū Bakr. A stooped man with sunken cheeks, a thin face, and deep-set eyes, Abū Bakr was an influential figure in Meccan public life who introduced five other leading citizens to Islam. Eventually these individuals became known as Muhammad's six companions. In later years their recollections of the prophet formed an important foundation for Islamic lore.

Muhammad Becomes More Aggressive

In A.D. 614, with a small band of disciples for encouragement, the Prophet became bolder in his public pronouncements. Now he verbally attacked idol worshippers and other pilgrims as they visited their favorite deities at the Kaaba. They were wrong, Muhammad insisted, for not worshipping the one true god, Allah.

Muhammad's newest round of religious pronouncements made a double impact: Many Meccans were offended, but others became interested in what he had to say. Those most sympathetic to his message tended to be poor, simple people who were dissatisfied with their own lives. They welcomed Muhammad's insistence that the rich share their wealth with the needy. In addition, like most Arabs, these converts had always believed that human existence ended with death. But Muhammad brought a new hope to their drab lives; the promise of a reward in an afterlife convinced them that they were better off following Allah than one of the many other gods.

Day by day Islam gained in strength and popularity. And as it did so, it also provoked a firestorm of dangerous hostility toward the Prophet.

Muhammad began preaching his creed in Mecca about A.D. 610, launching the spread of Islam throughout the Arabian Peninsula.

Arab Opposition to Muhammad

Some of Muhammad's opponents considered his denial of the existence of the many gods that were worshipped in the Kaaba to be blasphemous, or irreverent. Others were angry that increasing numbers of conversions to Islam were causing strife among clans and families. Even more disturbing, as far as the affluent Quraysh were concerned, was Muhammad's criticism that the wealthy ruling class had abandoned the traditional Bedouin and pre-Islamic practice of sharing with the poor.

Muhammad's enemies were also convinced that his public attacks on idol worshippers and pilgrims drove away cash-carrying visitors and hurt the local economy.

"Quraysh elders who held concessions to sell ritual robes, 'sacred' food, and water saw their profits shrink," writes author Edward Jurji. "The democratic spirit of Mohammed's[Muhammad's] preaching threatened the power of the upper classes. Thus town leaders turned in fury against [him]."[10]

Although violence, as a means of settling disputes and eliminating threats, was common in ancient Arabia, Muhammad was safe from physical attacks thanks to his uncle, Abū Talib, a leader of the Hashimite clan and a powerful and respected man in Mecca, who protected the Prophet and his followers. Moreover, Mecca was a holy city and a sanctuary, where Arabs were expected to avoid bloodshed. In addition, many of Muhammad's enemies were reluctant to attack him because they feared starting a blood feud, which were so common among desert tribes.

Nonetheless, Muhammad suffered. He endured endless slander and ridicule. The Quraysh also imposed a public ban on his family and him, which cut off their food and supplies. These necessities had to be delivered in secret by friends and followers.

Unable to physically punish Muhammad, many of his enemies took out their wrath by beating and stoning Meccan slaves who converted to Islam. Some were cast into jail or forced to stand uncovered in the lethal rays of the desert sun. Though slaves were not protected by ancient tribal law from such harassment, they were considered equals under Islam. Thus, Abū Bakr felt compelled to use much of his personal wealth to buy the freedom of many of them. But these individuals often still faced persecution once they became free. At last Muhammad advised them to emigrate to Abyssinia, now Ethiopia, a country that offered them refuge. Any sorrow he may have felt at their departure only worsened as his luck soon turned for the worse.

Muhammad's Life Changes

The year 619 brought great grief to Muhammad. His beloved wife Khadījah died. So did his uncle Abū Talib. With his most powerful defender gone, Muhammad feared for his safety. He sought refuge in Tarif, a nearby town. But he was not welcomed there. Instead, the local population, not wanting to antagonize the powerful Quraysh, stoned him and drove him away.

A Child Bride Remembers

In Robert Payne's History of Islam, *Aishah offers her personal recollection of her childhood marriage to the Prophet.*

"I was six years old when the Prophet betrothed himself to me in Mecca. Three years later in Madinah [Medina], I being nine years old, had a fever and lost my hair, but it had all grown again long and thick. One day I was on a swing surrounded by children friends. My mother came and called me, I did not know what for. I went to her. I was out of breath, and she made me stop at the door until I got my breath back. She then washed my head and face with some water, and took me to a room where there were some Ansar women, who cried out: 'Happiness and blessing and best fortune be upon thee!' My mother handed me over to them and they dressed me up. They had scarcely finished when the Prophet entered suddenly. They gave me over to him."

Bloodied and bruised from the stoning, Muhammad returned to Mecca, now a lonely man of fifty and living a precarious existence. Eventually, though, he remarried, taking two wives, as polygamy was permissible in Arab culture.

Despite the threats against him, Muhammad continued to preach. According to Muslim tradition, during this time Muhammad miraculously traveled on a night journey from Mecca to Jerusalem. Then he is said to have ascended into heaven and witnessed its divine glories. Many years later the sacred shrine of Islam, the Dome of the Rock, was built on the site in Jerusalem where Muhammad is believed to have arrived during the night journey. This location is also sacred to Jews, who believe that here Abraham once proved his loyalty to God by preparing to sacrifice his son.

The Rise of Medina

One day a group of pilgrims in Mecca heard Muhammad and were impressed with his sermons. At the time their own town of Yathrib, later known as Medina, which lay 250 miles to the north, was torn by strife and disorder. Unlike barren Mecca, Medina was located in a prosperous farming area that was founded by Jewish tribes. "The city lacked any stable authority," writes historian Joel Carmichael. "It was kept in a state of explosive division by the clan rivalries of two great Arab tribes, with the Jews acting only as counterweights in the fluctuating balance of power." [11]

The merchants became convinced that Muhammad was just the authority figure Medina needed to settle disputes. And his religious views would present no serious problem, they reasoned. After all, the people of Medina were long accustomed to the Jewish faith. At the moment Muhammad's preachings did not seem radically different. In fact some of Medina's Jewish leaders even thought Muhammad could be the messiah, or savior, who their ancient prophets had predicted would one day come.

Thus, the town leaders of Medina dispatched a group of men with a message to Muhammad officially inviting him to come and rule them. Several of the men swore loyalty to him on the spot. "We shall worship only the One God," they promised. "We shall not steal, nor commit adultery, nor kill our children; we shall not commit acts of slander; and we shall not disobey the Apostle of God in anything that is proper." [12]

Tempting as the offer was, however, Muhammad did not readily accept it.

The sacred shine of Islam, the Dome of the Rock. The shrine was built on the site in Jerusalem where Muhammad is said to have ascended into heaven.

Wary of what might await him in a strange town, he instead sent one of his followers to preach in Medina. Then he ordered his more than two hundred disciples to quietly begin emigrating from Mecca, one by one, to Medina. There they were to await his eventual arrival.

At last the only two Muslims left in Mecca were Muhammad and Abū Bakr. But in 622, the two men learned of something that hastened their own swift departure: a secret plot to murder the Prophet.

The Flight of Muhammad

The steady migration of Muslims to Medina alarmed the Quraysh elders. They feared that if the revolutionary prophet took charge of an important town, especially one located on the caravan route to Syria, he could pose a serious threat to Mecca. Muhammad, they decided, had to be stopped, despite previous qualms they had over shedding blood in Mecca.

"They arranged that he should be murdered in his bed; and in order to share the guilt of this breach of sanctuary [sacred place] they appointed a committee to do this, representing every family in the city except Muhammad's own," writes English author H. G. Wells. [13]

According to Muslim tradition, Muhammad learned in a revelation from Allah that his life was in danger in Mecca. He was also notified by an informer about the murder plan. Along with Abū Bakr, Muhammad fled to the cave of Thaur located not far from Mecca. He left behind, according to one version of the story, his adopted son 'Alī, who slept in the Prophet's room in an attempt to mislead

Mischievous Desert Spirits

In his book, Fabled Cities, Princes and Jinn from Arab Myths and Legends, *Khairat Al-Saleh provides this description of the jinn and their role in the spiritual realm of the ancient Arab world.*

"To the ancient Arabs, the jinn represented the hostile, unsympathetic forces of nature. They inspired such fear and awe in the minds of the Bedouin that some tribes worshipped them and offered them sacrifices to win their favour.

After Islam, belief in the existence of the jinn persisted; they were seen not as deities [gods], but as creatures representing a separate, alien state of being. According to legend and folklore, the jinn can usually appear in any shape or form they choose: human or animal. The more malicious among them favour the forms of beetles, toads, bats, scorpions and goats and especially snakes (though household serpents are believed to be good rather than bad jinn.) Some jinn keep the shape of animals permanently, particularly those of wild black dogs."

his enemies about Muhammad's whereabouts.

The two men eluded their hunters for three days. Then on July 16, 622 of the western or Gregorian calendar, they began a two-hundred-mile camel ride to the north until they reached Medina, where a throng of jubilant Muslims cheered their arrival.

This flight, or Hegira, of Muhammad proved to be an important turning point in the development of Islam. In fact, seventeen years later a powerful Muslim leader proclaimed the first day of the Hegira as the start of year one of a calendar still used today throughout the Muslim world. (Because this calendar is based on the movements of the moon rather than the sun, the Arab-Muslim year is shorter than one based on 365¼ solar days. Use of the lunar calendar also means that the Muslim religious holy month occurs at slightly different times each year.)

The Hegira also marked the start of a new chapter in the history of humanity. The rule of Muhammad had begun.

Chapter

2 The Fundamentals of a New Faith

Although Muhammad had escaped to Medina without bodily harm, he knew the prospect of war with Mecca remained strong, if not inevitable. But to unify his followers for possible battle, he first had to solve internal problems within the exiled Muslim community. When the refugees, or *muhajirin*, left Mecca, they severed all family, clan, and tribal ties. The tearing of these traditional bonds dispirited and worried the Muslims. They had always relied on these familial connections to protect them in a dangerous desert world.

Creating a Brotherhood

Adding to the Muslim's woes was the problem of open jealousy that had erupted between the refugees and the natives of Medina who had converted to Muhammad's teachings, known as the helpers, or *ansar*. Many helpers believed that as newly converted Muslims they had to compete with the refugees to receive equal standing in Muhammad's eyes. This split among his followers, Muhammad soon realized, threatened to make all Muslims perilously vulnerable if the Quraysh ever attacked. He set out to weld his believers together.

Muhammad's first important act was to alter his role as leader. "While in Mecca he had been merely the religious leader of a small group, somewhat in the tradition of the earlier Hebrew prophets," writes author Desmond Stewart. "But once settled in Medina he played a new and more powerful role, with increasing spiritual and political authority."[14] Now, in addition to being a religious leader, Muhammad had to act like a statesman, politician, judge, and king all rolled into one. With his new and enhanced authority, he decided to solidify his followers into a group which shared values. As the settlement's central force, he created a new community, or *umma*, of brotherhood among all his followers. A document now known as the Constitution of Medina officially established a union among four different Arab groups. Jews, who inhabited the town and generally did not accept Muhammad as their prophet, were given secondary status.

To strengthen a spirit of brotherhood between the refugees and the helpers, Muhammad commanded that a member of each group be paired with someone of the opposing group to work as friends and comrades.

All Muslims were equal, he declared. Exploitation of the weak was forbidden. To stress these ideas, Muhammad led by

THE FUNDAMENTALS OF A NEW FAITH ■ 23

example. Though he was leader of the *umma*, he refused to be treated as royalty. He avoided appearing aloof and apart from his disciples. He wore simple garb. He mingled openly with fellow Muslims of all levels. He often did his own household chores in a common clay house, not a palace.

Muhammad's effort at community building paid off. It helped to ease the tension between the various factions of believers and to unite believers for protection. In the process, seeds were sown for a major social change that eventually changed everyday life in Arabia. Until the *umma*, family blood ties both united the members of a particular tribe and separated them from others. Through the creation of the *umma*, though, a new force emerged that cemented tribes together and reduced strife among them: religious faith.

Following his arrival in Medina, Muhammad continued to receive divine revelations. Increasingly, however, these visions tended to express political and social ideas rather than religious ones.

One day Muhammad held a religious ceremony attended by all Muslims. "Allah is most great!" he proclaimed. The throng echoed his words. At one point during his sermon, Muhammad descended from the pulpit, lay with his face on the ground, and prayed. This public gesture, which he performed three times, set forth an example that his followers have imitated ever since. The act of prostrating oneself, or lying flat, in public, Muhammad explained, symbolized a total surrender to God's will. In fact, the word *Islam* literally means to surrender; a Muslim is one who surrenders.

Such a surrender, Muhammad said, was part of a divine plan that was clearly evident in the natural world. "Fish, birds, animals, flowers, mountains and winds do not have choice about whether or not they submit to the divine plan," explains Karen Armstrong. "They express God's will for them in each moment of their existence."[15] Muhammad implored his disciples to surrender their lives in a like manner.

Muhammad Builds a New Society

Muhammad became more than a spiritual leader. He also became the *umma*'s chief judge and lawgiver. In the world of Islam there is no clear separation of religion and government, as is the case in most Western nations. Instead, Muhammad imposed upon Medina a theocracy, or rule by a religious leader. Under his command the realms of religion and the power of the state were deliberately combined. As both lawgiver and religious leader, Muhammad regularly sought guidance from his visions. Allah, said Muhammad, expected members of the *umma* to demonstrate the same level of equality, generosity, and graciousness as they would to family members. And God also "forbids evil designs, ill-behavior and transgression. He admonishes you that you may take heed."[16]

Muhammad also wanted to impose a clear-cut system of right and wrong for his followers to adhere to. For this to happen he turned to *muruwah*, which was the old tribal code of the Arabs. *Muruwah* emphasized the good of the group over individual rights. It also stressed cooperation and providing care for the poor, the weak, and the needy.

Arabs at noon prayer. The man on the far right prostrates himself, a practice begun by Muhammad to symbolize total surrender to God.

"Muhammad's chief innovation was to extend these principles to include all Muslims, to the entire *umma* rather than to just the members of the single tribe," writes Karen Armstrong.[17]

Unable to read or write himself, or at least not well, Muhammad dictated from memory what he took to be revelations from God. He knew that his people were more apt to obey Islamic laws if they understood they came from God.

Dutifully his disciples copied down his words on scraps of parchment, palm leaves, leather, or whatever they could find. Many Muslims memorized his utterances—eventually some seventy-eight thousand words—and considered them sacred and incapable of error. Collectively Muhammad's sayings became the Koran, the basic text for a faith revered by millions.

Islam's Holy Book

However, the Koran was not actually compiled into one volume until after the death of Muhammad. Abū Bakr, the Prophet's first successor, or caliph, ordered all fragments containing Muhammad's revealed holy words to be collected and preserved in book form. Muhammad's second successor, Caliph 'Umar, ordered Muslims to collect every word "whether inscribed on date-leaves, shreds of leather, shoulder-blades, stone tablets or the hearts of man."[18]

But at the time of these collections there was a problem; written Arabic contained no vowels or special markings for consonants. Thus, controversy arose over what some of the written words meant. A third successor, 'Uthmān, solved this problem by leading an effort to have scholars produce a standardized version of the Koran. He also ordered all other versions to be destroyed. Today 'Uthmān's rendition of the Koran remains the official version read around the world.

Muslims consider the Koran the most sacred and important religious work on earth. It differs from all other major religious works in that it is the product of only one man: Muhammad. Around the world Muslims and others continue to be astonished by the beauty, poetry, and noble quality of thought expressed in this religious work. Many scholars, in fact,

Devotion to the Koran is an essential part of Islamic life. This ornate page is from a thirteenth-century Koran.

consider the Koran the greatest literary masterpiece in the Arabic tongue.

Written in 114 verses, which are combined into chapters, or suras, the Koran contains commandments, rules, regulations, ethical pronouncements, historical accounts, and wise sayings. Muhammad also conveyed many edicts on justice, property, personal and family behavior, and responsibilities.

Since Muhammad's revelations occurred on an irregular basis over several decades, the ideas on which Islam was based also appeared in a fragmented fashion. As a result, the Koran is not arranged by theme or chronological order. Instead, the suras appear in order of decreasing length. But Muhammad's earliest utterances tended to be shorter than those at the end of his life. This means that the sayings appear roughly in reverse chronological order.

An unswerving belief and devotion to the Koran is essential to all Muslims. As children they memorize Koranic verses. Business deals between Muslims are consummated with recitations from the Koran. Its verses are recited at marriages; Koranic words are embroidered on green cloths, which are draped on white-shrouded corpses at funerals.

The Hadith

Muslims also derive spiritual nourishment and daily guidance from another holy book, a supplement to the Koran called the Hadith. Unlike the Koran, the Hadith contains the voices of many people, including those followers and companions who recalled the Prophet's sayings and his deeds. These accounts provide much of what religious scholars refer to as the tradition of Islam. This revered body of information contains an abundance of professed beliefs and social practices that provided a blueprint for the culture that accompanied the rise of Islam.

The Five Pillars

The basics of Islam appear in the Koran as simple and direct edicts called the Five Pillars of Islam. Each Muslim must adhere to each of them.

The first pillar, and the most important, is a *shahada*, or profession of faith.

Each Muslim must profess these words: "I testify there is no god but Allah, and Muhammad is his prophet."

Thus, a believer affirms the reality of one God and demolishes the possible existence of any rival gods represented by the idols at the Kaaba. And as for Muhammad, this profession of faith certifies a Muslim's recognition of God's chief agent on earth.

The next in importance is *salat*, or prayer. Believers must purify themselves with either water or desert sand and pray five times a day—morning, noon, midafternoon, after sunset, and before going to sleep—while facing Mecca, the Holy City. Even the Muslim dead are buried in such a way that they face Mecca.

When prayer time comes during the day, Muslims recite special verses, kneel, and prostrate themselves. If they are at home or work and unable to attend a mosque, or Muslim church, they are ex-

The Nature of Allah

The second major entry in the Quran, *as translated by Muhammad Zafrulla Khan, contains these lines, which were revealed to Muhammad after he completed the Hegira.*

"In the name of Allah, Most Gracious, Ever Merciful.
I AM ALLAH, THE ALL-KNOWING.
This is the Perfect Book, free from all doubt; it is a guidance for the righteous, who believe in the unseen, observe Prayer, and spend out of whatsoever We have bestowed upon them; and who believe in that which has been revealed to thee, and in that which was revealed before thee, and have firm faith in that which has been foretold and is yet to come. It is these who are firmly grounded in the guidance that has come from their Lord, and it is these who shall prosper. Those who have disbelieved so that it is the same whether thou warn them or warn them not, will not believe. Allah has set a seal on their hearts and their ears, and over their eyes there is a covering. For them there is a great punishment. . . .

Of the people there are some who say: We believe in Allah and the Last Day; yet they do not believe at all. They seek to deceive Allah and those who believe, but in truth they deceive none save themselves; only they perceive it not. In their minds is a disease; Allah through the continuous manifestation of His Signs causes their disease to grow worse. For them there is a painful punishment because of their lying."

pected to find a clean place or use a special prayer rug. In major Muslim cities a prayer caller, or muezzin, ascends a minaret, a tower that looms above a mosque, and calls believers to prayer. In recent years high-powered amplification systems broadcast the calls to prayer.

On Friday, which to Muslims is the most important day of the week, believers gather at mosques for formal religious services, group prayers, and recitations from the Koran.

Sawn, or fasting, is the third pillar. The purpose of the fast is to commemorate Muhammad's Hegira to Medina. Fasting is also expected to instill self-discipline and compassion in Muslims. No Muslim is allowed to eat, drink, smoke, or take medicine during daylight hours in the month of Ramadan, the Islamic month when God revealed himself to Muhammad. Some of the very devout have even refused to swallow their own saliva during this time. Every night during Ramadan, however, families and friends gather for huge meals. A festive holiday takes place at the end of Ramadan.

The next requirement is the giving of alms. This pillar, *zakat*, recognizes the fact that the poor in any society need help. Muhammad proclaimed that each Muslim, except the very poor, was required to contribute a portion of his or her wealth—about 2½ percent—to the poor, the needy, slaves trying to buy their freedom, debtors, and strangers.

The last pillar requires of every Muslim who is economically and physically able to make a pilgrimage, or *hajj*, to Mecca, the Holy City, at least once in a lifetime. At a special time each year Muslims, as they have for centuries, arrive in Mecca from around the world to take part in the religious observance. Pilgrims dress in white to acknowledge their sameness and equality before Allah. This mass assemblage of believers—Arabs, Turks, Indonesians, Persians, and members of many other ethnic groups and nationalities—congregate at the Kaaba for several days and take part in a variety of rituals and practices similar to those in pre-Islamic times.

The five pillars of the faith include prayer five times a day. This Muslim kneels on a prayer rug during his morning prayer.

Religious pilgrims camp in front of the walls of Mecca, which houses the Kaaba, the holiest Islamic shrine. Islamic law dictates that all able Muslims must make at least one journey to Mecca.

The One True God

The main purpose of Islam is to worship Allah. But what is Allah like? In many ways the Islamic interpretation of the nature of God is similar to that found in the Christian Old Testament, or Hebrew Bible. The Koran portrays Allah, the creator and master of everything, as an awesome cosmic power—one who gives out vengeance to the wayward, the pagan, the idol worshipper. "He is Allah, the Single; Allah, the Self-Existing and Besought of all. He begets not, nor is He begotten; and there is none equal to Him in his attributes."[19]

Being all-powerful and all knowing, Allah knows the fate, or predestiny, of everyone and everything. "This belief in predestination made fatalism a prominent feature in Moslem thought," writes Will Durant. "It was used by Mohammad and other leaders to encourage bravery in battle, since no danger could hasten, nor any

caution defer, the predestined hour of each man's death."[20]

Muhammad believed that Allah inspired a series of earlier Jewish prophets, all mentioned in the Bible—Adam, Noah, Abraham, Moses, Enoch, and Christ—to reveal his divine purposes on earth. According to Muhammad, Adam was not the first man on earth. Rather, he was the first human who was spiritually developed enough to receive Allah's revelations. Muhammad also considered himself the last of the prophets.

The Prophet also taught that even though Christian and Jewish scriptures were divinely inspired, they had been altered so much over the many centuries that they could no longer be trusted. Only the Koran, he said, remained as the uncorrupted word of God.

"Muhammad maintained that he did not bring a new message from a new God," writes scholar John L. Esposito, "but called people back to the one, true God

A European's View of Mecca

Englishman Sir Richard Burton numbered among the handful of nineteenth-century European adventurers who violated Islamic law by masquerading as Muslims and secretly making the journey to Mecca. This excerpt of Burton's written account, Pilgrimage to Al-Madina and Meccah, 1855, *appears in Desmond Stewart's* Mecca *and offers a firsthand look at the diverse mass of humanity that flowed into the Holy City one moonlit night.*

"The oval pavement round the Ka'abah [Kaaba] was crowded with men, women, and children, mostly divided into parties: some walking staidly, and others running, whilst many stood in groups to prayer. What a scene of contrasts! Here stalked the Badawi woman, in her long black robe like a nun's serge, and poppy-coloured face-veil, pierced to show two fiercely flashing orbs [eyes]. There an Indian woman, with her semi-Tartar features, nakedly hideous, and her thin legs, encased in wrinkled tights, hurried round the fane [shrine]. Every now and then a corpse borne upon its wooden shell, circuited the shrine by means of four bearers, whom other Moslems [Muslims], as is the custom, occasionally relieved. A few fair-skinned Turks lounged about, looking cold and repulsive, as their wont is. In one place a [visitor from India] stood, with turban awry and arms akimbo, contemplating the view jauntily, as those 'gentlemen's gentlemen' will do. In another, some poor wretch, with arms thrown on high, so that every part of his person might touch the Ka'abah, was clinging to the curtain and sobbing as though his heart would break."

Throngs of worshippers converge on the Great Mosque in Mecca for a midday prayer. The Kaaba can be seen in the courtyard of the mosque.

and to a way of life that most of his contemporaries had forgotten or deviated from."[21]

The Koranic Universe

Muslims believe in a three-dimensional universe: heaven, earth, and hell. This universe is populated with humans, angels, and the trouble-making jinns. Satan is also present. Islam often portrays Satan not only as a symbol of ultimate evil, but also as an arrogant, misguided spirit and a trivializer of God's blessing.

Like Christians, Muslims believe there will be both a final judgment day and a resurrection of souls. The dead will sleep until this final reckoning. Then Allah will review each individual's Book of Deeds to determine the afterlife of all humans. A book placed in the right hand of each individual on judgment day means the Muslim is rewarded with heaven; a book appearing in the left signifies damnation and everlasting punishment in hell.

Allah is ultimately good, kind, and merciful to those who worship him. Therefore he rewards virtuous believers. Heaven, the Garden of Paradise, is a place of inspiring beauty, eternal youth, and extreme pleasure that awaits the souls that Allah favors. Here, according to the Koran, are "Gardens beneath . . . which rivers flow . . . "[22] and "rivers of milk . . . and rivers of wine . . . and rivers of pure honey."[23]

Hell, though, is a region of horror. "For those who deny the Hour We have prepared a blazing fire. . . ," Allah reveals in the Koran. "When they are thrown into a narrow corner thereof, chained together, they will at once pray for annihila-tion."[24] Worse yet, the doomed "will taste therein neither coolness nor any pleasant drink save boiling water and a nauseating fluid."[25]

With such punishment awaiting wayward believers, Muslims are taught not only to love and respect Allah, but also to have *taqwa*, or fear, of God. However, say some, those who roast in hell may not be there eternally. Perhaps, Allah will release them. After all, "Thy Lord does whatever He pleases."[26]

Islamic Behavior

Islam also involves a host of laws, rules, and customs that determine a specific code of behavior. Muslims, for instance, may not eat pork. This prohibition makes sense in a hot climate where pork quickly spoils. Decaying pork often carries the parasite trichina, which causes fever and muscular pain. Muhammad also forbade the drinking of alcoholic beverages. This ban conformed well with preexisting Arab custom. Public drunkenness or other disorderly behavior has long been discouraged by Arabs. In addition, gambling and the worship of idols were banned by Muhammad. He also abolished the ancient desert-dwelling practice of killing unwanted babies. Although he did not rid Arabic society of the ancient practice of slavery, he did reveal to his followers that freeing slaves was a virtuous act. Moreover, he implored masters to treat slaves humanely. Slaves, the Prophet proclaimed, were now permitted to marry and to purchase their liberty.

Muhammad strengthened the bonds of marriage as well. Allah, he said, blessed matrimony. Violation of marital vows displeased him. The Koran allowed a Muslim man to take four wives, providing he could care for and treat each of them equally. Muhammad, however, was exempt from the Koranic rule. After the death of his first wife, Khadījah, over twenty years the Prophet eventually took ten wives. Such polygamy, however, is often misunderstood in the West. Because the ancient Arab world was filled with violence and strife, many men were doomed to lead short lives. The resulting scarcity of marriageable men meant trouble for single women, for an unmarried woman in the Arabian desert was, and still is, an unprotected person. Thus, marriage became a form of security for women. Many of Muhammad's wives, for instance, were widows of men fallen in battle. One was Aishah, the seven-year-old daughter of Abū Bakr.

Perched in a tall tower, or minaret, a muezzin calls to Muslim worshippers, "Come to prayer! Come to prayer!"

The Importance of Prayer

Each day Muslims ritually wash themselves—their hair, face, and arms up to the elbows, and feet up to the ankles—in order to cleanse themselves physically and to pave the way for the purification of the soul, which had to be done by prayer. A Muslim's first prayer each day is an individual morning prayer. Four others follow during the course of the day, the last being at nightfall.

Rather than a Christian bell or a Jewish ram's horn to call the faithful to prayer, Muslims responded to the call of a muezzin, the prayer caller who from a housetop or tower erupted with this cry to worship:

Allah akbar! [God is greater!] *Allahu akbar!*
I testify there is no god but God!
I testify that Muhammad is the Messenger of God!
Come to prayer! Come to prayer!
Come to salvation! Come to salvation!
Allahu akbar! Allahu akbar!
No god there is, but God![27]

Muslims were allowed to pray individually wherever they happened to be during the day at the prescribed times. But once a week they were required to congregate in a mosque, a building used for religious worship and which was fashioned after Muhammad's home in Medina. Here, as a group, Muslims prayed or chanted verses from the Koran together. They were led in these acts by an imam, or prayer leader, who might also provide a sermon or lecture on religious themes.

Such group prayer sessions symbolized, in part, the Islamic teaching that all Muslim believers are equal. Racism played no part. A common sight throughout the Muslim world was that of Arabs, Syrians, African blacks, Persians, Europeans, and Muslims from other lands and cultures mingling freely and equally in marketplaces.

Women, however, were an exception to the rule.

Women Under Islam

Although Islam promised women equality, they generally were expected to be subservient to men. Many devout Muslim women dressed modestly and wore veils across their faces to conceal their beauty.

Generally they tended to the affairs of the home rather than those of the public world. In many places in the Muslim world this custom, called purdah, became common. Often purdah was misunderstood by those outside of the Islamic world, who dismissed it as a form of slavery. However, from the Muslim point of view, what purdah provided was a form of protection for women from lawless bandits by secluding them at home. Many Muslims also believed the custom helped to limit women's opportunities to be tempted into extramarital relations.

Although Muslim women seldom achieved the same status as men, many modern scholars caution observers in the West not to be too harsh in condemning Islam for its treatment of women. In fact, they point out, Muhammad did much to improve the status of women during his reign. Before Islam, writes Huston Smith,

A Prayerful Asking

In Huston Smith's The Religions of Man *appears this traditional prayer that a Muslim is likely to recite each day.*

"O Lord! Grant me firmness in faith and direction. Assist me in being grateful to Thee and in adoring Thee in every good way. I ask Thee for an innocent heart, which shall not incline to wickedness. I ask Thee for a true tongue. I pray Thee to defend me from that vice which Thou knowest, and for forgiveness of those faults which Thou knowest. O my Defender! assist me in remembering Thee and being grateful to Thee, and in worshipping Thee with the excess of my strength. Forgive me out of Thy loving kindness, and have mercy on me; for verily Thou art the forgiver of offences and the bestower of blessings on Thy servant."

"Women were regarded as little more than chattel [property] to be done with as their fathers or husbands pleased. Daughters had no inheritance rights and were often buried alive in their infancy."[28]

With Muhammad, however, Arabian women for the first time in history had a leader who proclaimed they were entitled to certain rights. The Prophet, for instance, declared that women had the same legal standing as men. During pre-Islamic times parents of daughters who married received a bridal gift, or dowry, from the groom's family. But under Islamic law this gift belonged to the bride herself. Women could inherit property, and in some Muslim lands they were allowed to open a business, keep the profits, and pursue any profession open to men.

Divorce

The Koran absorbed and continued the pre-Islamic practices of divorce. All that was required of a Muslim man wanting to divorce his wife was to state aloud these words three times: "Thou are dismissed." However, a man should not act hastily, for once a divorce took place, he could not quickly remarry his former wife if he had a change of heart. This safeguard was set up to discourage a man from surrendering to his temper too quickly.

A Muslim woman, on the other hand, could not divorce her husband, unless she gave back her dowry to him. However, Islamic law did enable a woman to demand freedom from marriage if her husband took another wife.

Although divorce was permitted, Muhammad discouraged the practice. Al-lah, he said, was not pleased by it. The Prophet, in fact, encouraged unhappy couples to work out their differences with the help of negotiators from each family.

The Koran also frowns on adultery. Once, the punishment for men and women sinners alike was severe: to be flogged one hundred times. Muhammad softened this practice, though, when local gossips whispered that his wife Aishah, when she was grown, had been unfaithful. Subsequently, Muhammad had another revelation of a new law that required from that point onward any accusers to produce four witnesses to testify that a woman had sinned. Failure to do so when bringing charges against "honorable women," said Muhammad, would earn the accusers a "flogging with eighty stripes [blows]." Furthermore, they would never be able to offer testimony again. "Accusations of adultery thereafter were rare," observes Will Durant.[29]

Islamic Unity

Many of Islam's edicts may seem harsh and demanding to modern non-Muslims. But they served early Muslims well. Islam provided consistent standards and rules that gave Arabs security, stability, and a sense of unity that sustained them through the travails of everyday life in a hostile environment. The religion also gave Muslims hope and spiritual nourishment in a turbulent time of change and uncertainty in Arabic history. This youngest of world religions also furnished Muslims with the all-purpose unity they needed to wield great power beyond their borders and their wildest imaginings.

3 The Conquests of Islam

In Mecca, Muhammad had been a prophet, a lone voice spreading a divine message. But in Medina, at age fifty-one, he found himself a powerful religious and political figure who commanded great power and respect among the *umma*. Blood ties traditionally had been the social glue that held tribes together in Arabia. But the *umma* that Muhammad created relied on a new type of bond that centered on religious faith rather than tribal loyalty. The community wrought by Muhammad at Medina became the standard for all future Muslim societies.

Muhammad introduced another important lasting change in Arabic life. In pre-Islamic times important tribal decisions were usually made by a group of tribal elders who tried to reach agreement before taking action. In the *umma*, on the other hand, Muhammad, who acted in the name of Allah, was an autocrat. That is, he

In Medina, Muhammad established a Muslim community from which he received great respect and loyalty. Here, Muhammad preaches to faithful followers.

made such decisions alone. Perhaps only a theocracy, or government run by a religious leader, such as Muhammad's was powerful enough to overcome the ancient feuds and hostilities that existed among the various Arabian tribes. Future Muslim leaders would follow his autocratic example in the centuries ahead.

Muslim Raids

The *umma* faced serious economic problems during its early days. The presence of the two hundred refugees who migrated to Medina increased the demand for resources and soon caused a food shortage in that city. Because they had left their homes and businesses back in Mecca, the refugees lacked the financial resources needed to sustain themselves in their adopted town. The hard-pressed faithful turned to their new leader for help. Muhammad responded by ordering his men to launch a series of raids against caravans headed for Mecca. Four-fifths of the booty went to the raiders, he proclaimed; the remaining one-fifth Muhammad kept for the good of the community.

Robbing desert travelers was not uncommon in the Arab world of the seventh century. Bedouins, in fact, had routinely made such raids for centuries. Nonetheless, Arabs everywhere reacted angrily when Muslims attacked a caravan and killed a man during the month of Rajab, a sacred month with a time-honored ban on violence.

And when the Muslims' continued raids on caravans began to hurt Mecca economically, Quraysh leaders vowed to punish Muhammad and his followers. They soon had their chance in March 624.

Desert travel was a dangerous occupation in the Arab world. In the seventh century under Muhammad's command, Muslim warriors launched a series of raids on desert caravans.

An Execution

In Karen Armstrong's Muhammad: A Biography of the Prophet, *Aishah recalls the final moments in the life of a woman whom Muslims executed with more than six hundred Banu-Kuraiza Jewish men:*

"She was actually with me and was talking with me and laughing immoderately as the apostle was killing her men in the market when suddenly an unseen voice called her name.
'Good heavens,' I cried, 'What is the matter?'
'I am to be killed,' she replied.
'What for?' I asked.
'Because of something I did,' she answered. She was taken away and beheaded. . . . I shall never forget my wonder at her good spirits and her loud laughter when all the time she knew that she would be killed."

When Muhammad learned that a caravan bearing a bounty of goods was passing near Medina, he ordered his 315 men to prepare for an attack. He lost the element of surprise, though, when Abū Sufyan, a merchant who commanded the caravan learned of the coming attack and changed course. Then Abū Sufyan sent an appeal for help to the Quraysh, who sent back more than 900 armed Meccans to defend and escort the caravan home.

The two small armies headed for a collision at Wad Badr, a dry riverbed about twenty miles south of Medina. As they neared each other, Meccan leader Abū Jahl boasted of victory to his men: "We shall spend three days in Badr, slaughter camels, feast and drink wine. We shall have girls to play for us, and the Arabs will hear that we have gathered together and show respect for us." [30]

Meanwhile, the Muslims felt equally confident. Muhammad assured his men, "Not one who fights this day and bears himself with steadfast courage . . . shall meet his death without Allah bringing him to paradise." [31]

Muhammad's forces won at Badr that day and proclaimed their victory as sign of God's favoritism. They returned to Medina loaded with booty and prisoners. Some of the captives were held for ransom; others, especially those who had persecuted Muslims in Mecca, were killed. These killings, however, did not satisfy the Muslim's lust for revenge. Next they hunted down well-known critics of Muhammad and killed them. This purge included any Jews in Medina who had ridiculed the Prophet's explanations of the Bible and his claim to be the messiah. Until now Muhammad had believed that he was continuing to add to the basic religious truths proclaimed by Jewish prophets long before. But now he changed his mind. Inspired by a new revelation, Muhammad accused Jews of falsifying holy scriptures and punished any Jews still alive with exile.

Then Muhammad announced a startling new decree. No longer were Muslims to honor Jerusalem as the *qibla*, the holy place to face when praying. From this time onward they were to face Mecca. With this change in ritual, Islam became a full-bodied *Arab* religion.

"The change of the *qibla* has been called Muhammad's most creative religious gesture," writes Karen Armstrong. "In turning towards Mecca, Muslims were tacitly [silently] declaring that they belonged to none of the established communities, but were turning only towards God himself."[32]

Trouble Continues to Brew

Hostilities continued between Mecca and Medina. A major confrontation took place in 625, when Abū Sufyan led a force of three thousand Meccans against Muhammad's men at Ohod, a hill near Medina. This time it was the Muslims who suffered a military setback. One of the casualties from the fighting that day was Muhammad himself. When the screaming and bloodletting of battle subsided, the Prophet lay blood soaked on the ground, with one eye hanging from its socket.

The defeat left the Prophet deeply troubled. How had they lost, he wondered. Why had they lost Allah's favor? After brooding over these vexing questions during his convalescence, Muhammad finally came up with an answer. Muslims, he concluded, had become too interested in the booty of war. They had forgotten about their duty to God.

Although the Prophet recovered enough to lead his people, his mood was dark. With vengeance in his heart, he accused a nearby Jewish encampment of helping the Meccan forces that had killed many Muslims and nearly slain him. He ordered his warriors to forcibly drive these Jews from their settlement near Medina and confiscate their homes and property. Despite his earlier misgivings, he then turned over these spoils of war to his loyal refugees. After all, they had left all their possessions in Mecca and were in dire need of property.

Two years passed before the Meccans and Muslims fought again. This time Meccans struck at Medina with an army of ten thousand warriors with the intention of smashing the Muslims once and for all.

But they were in for a surprise. Muhammad had taken unusual precautions to safeguard Medina. Acting on the advice of one of his men, he ordered a massive trench dug at the southeastern section of the town and a protective wall erected.

These obstacles both surprised and infuriated the Meccan warriors. They taunted Muhammad for hiding behind such barricades and not fighting in the traditional Bedouin manner. But Muhammad was untouched by their jeers.

His precautions paid off. Though the Meccans kept up their siege for several weeks, they failed to take the city. When powerful rains and wind blew onto the battlefield, the dispirited Meccans called off their attack and vanished.

Once more the Muslims felt betrayed. This time they rounded up another Jewish tribe—the Banu-Kuraiza Jews, whom the Muslims believed had provisioned the unsuccessful Meccans before the attack on Medina. Muhammad told the prisoners that another Arabic tribe, the Aus, and not he, would decide their punishment.

Many Muslims expected the Jews to be exiled and were taken aback when the Aus leader, a stern Muslim convert, declared, "I condemn the men to death, their property to be divided by the victors, their women and children to be slaves."[33]

Muhammad kept his word and ordered the death sentence carried out: his men slaughtered between six hundred and nine hundred Banu-Kuraiza men. The women and children were sold into slavery. Once again Muhammad ordered his men to confiscate Jewish land and divide it among his followers.

Yearning for Mecca

Despite all the profit, power, and glory gleaned from military success on behalf of their faith, many Muslims were unhappy. A long time had passed since they had last seen their relatives and friends in Mecca. Many also yearned to make a religious pilgrimage to the Kaaba, especially now that Mecca served as the new *qibla*.

Muhammad sympathized with his followers, and in 628 he set out with fourteen hundred Muslims to enter Mecca. Instead of using force, however, he brokered a deal with his enemy in Mecca: Muhammad offered to abide by a ten-year truce and call off the caravan raids if the Meccans allowed the Muslims to make a pilgrimage to Mecca unimpeded.

To Muhammad's surprise many Muslims were disappointed and angry that their leader had accepted such terms. By now they had grown accustomed to the plunder of war and the excitement of conquest. Their desire to attack Mecca had been frustrated by Muhammad's agreement.

Perhaps to appease his frustrated warriors, Muhammad allowed them to raid the Jewish oasis of Khybar, a three-day journey to the northeast. Here the Muslims killed ninety-three people before they accepted a Jewish surrender. Those who did give up were spared, but they were also forced to pay 50 percent of their annual earnings as tribute to the Muslims.

Muhammad's men need not have worried about not having Quraysh to fight, for the truce with Mecca was short-lived. In November 629 Muhammad announced that a desert tribe allied with Mecca had attacked Muslims. This action, he argued, justified his voiding the peace agreement. Accompanied by ten thousand Muslims, the Prophet went by camelback into Mecca in January 630 only to find no significant resistance from the forces of the Quraysh.

Thus, almost bloodlessly, Muslims took over the Holy City. Muhammad ordered the destruction of all idols at the Kaaba and rededicated it as a sacred shrine for Muslims. Mecca, he announced, was now the official Holy City of Islam. Entry to the town was forbidden to all nonbelievers upon penalty of death.

Not long afterwards Muhammad learned that some two hundred miles north of Mecca several Arabian tribes were angered by the Muslim action and vowed to defend their idols. Despite their proud words, they proved to be no match for the power of Muhammad's forces. Led by the Prophet, Muslim troops roared into rebel camps and easily crushed the uprisings.

Muhammad's Rule in Mecca

Muhammad now spent his days running the affairs of his new and growing em-

With the fall of Mecca (pictured) in 630, Muhammad became a powerful political figure. He continued launching raids and unifying desert tribes, stretching his empire across Arabia.

pire. Inspired by an apparently never ending flow of revelations, he addressed many social, economic, political, and legal problems confronting his people. His family—now enlarged by the acquisition of ten wives—also competed for his attention.

Muslim warrior-disciples, meanwhile, sought relentlessly to spread Islam far beyond the gates of Mecca and Medina. Bearing both swords and treaties, plus Koranic teachings, they descended upon one desert tribe after another. At first many of these nomadic tribes resisted Muhammad's teachings more vigorously than did town dwellers. "The Bedouins . . . were essentially interested in nothing so much as the delights of this life—fighting, drinking, gambling, and lovemaking," argues historian Joel Carmichael.[34] The new Islamic values imparted by Muhammad collided with their traditional ideas. At first the proud Bedouins obeyed the customs of their ancestors and therefore resisted the religious rules of Muhammad that required customary praying, almsgiving, and

avoiding alcohol. More troubling still was the Muslim emphasis on forgiveness, a concept that was at odds with the ancient Bedouin code of revenge.

"Failure to pay back an insult was regarded by the pre-Islamic Arab world . . . as a symptom of vulgar cowardice that covered the whole tribe with shame," Carmichael points out.[35]

Despite their misgivings about many of Muhammad's dictates, these desert dwellers did find one aspect of Muslim behavior to their liking, argues historian William H. McNeill. "[The Bedouins] were strongly attracted by the prospect of sharing in the booty which successful raiding expeditions so regularly brought in," he writes. "Moreover, as success followed success, it became obvious to all that God indeed favored the Moslem cause."[36]

Within a few years, wielding both persuasion and force, Muslim warriors overtook all but some of the most remote tribes in Arabia. Unquestionably, by 631 the lion's share of the peninsula clearly belonged to Muhammad and to Islam.

The Death of the Prophet

During Muhammad's fifty-ninth year in life, his health began to fail. Fever spells and headaches plagued him. These spells, which had lasted for years, apparently also altered his behavior. According to his wife Aishah, these bouts at times caused him to act strangely and to talk fatalistically of death.

On the morning of June 7, 632, the last day of his life, Muhammad joined believers for prayer in the mosque. He concluded the meeting with a poignant final message to his followers: "O men, the fire is kindled! Rebellions come like the darkness of the night! By God, you cannot lay these things to my charge! I allow what the Quran allows, and forbid what the Quran forbids!"[37]

The elderly Muhammad. His death in 632 shocked the Arab world, which chose Abū Bakr to succeed the prophet.

Then, complaining of a headache, Muhammad went to Aishah. As noon approached, he laid his head upon her breast. "Nay," she heard him say, "the most Exalted Companion in Paradise."[38] They were his last words on earth.

At first Aishah did not understand what had happened to her husband. "It was due to my ignorance and extreme youth that the apostle died in my arms," she later recalled.[39]

News of the Prophet's death shocked believers across Arabia. Muhammad himself had become the centerpiece of their faith and the symbol of their security and well-being. Without his presence many felt lost and abandoned. Others feared that without Muhammad's guidance the *umma* would disintegrate and Islam would vanish.

When panic began to mount within the community at Medina, Abū Bakr, Muhammad's companion and father of Aishah addressed a distraught crowd with blunt, strong, and yet spiritually moving language. "O men," he cried, "if anyone worships Muhammad, Muhammad is dead. If anyone worships God, God is alive, immortal."[40]

Then Abū Bakr read a verse Muhammad had revealed on an earlier occasion: "Muhammad is naught but a Messenger; Messengers have passed away before him. Why, if he should die or is slain, will you turn upon your heels? If any man should turn about on his heels, he will not harm God in any way; and God will recompense the Thankful."[41]

Abū Bakr's speech overwhelmed the crowd. His words brought a heartrending sense of finality. But he had also powerfully clarified that Muhammad, the man, and his divine message were not the same thing. Islam still lived. Allah's commands yet existed. Abū Bakr had shown them that the need to carry on with Islam was greater than the life of a man.

Despite Abū Bakr's calming words, Muslims still knew that a strong leader was needed to contain and guide the *umma*. Who would steer them now that the great Muhammad was gone? This question provoked spiritual and political crises that would last for centuries and ultimately divide and splinter Islam forever.

The Rule of Abū Bakr

Not one individual among the Muslims enjoyed the same stature or prestige as Muhammad. No one claimed to be another prophet of Allah. How could he? Had not Muhammad himself proclaimed that he himself was the last and greatest prophet? Even more troubling was the fact that Muhammad had no son to carry on his work. Nor had he set up a system for picking a successor after his death.

Muslims knew that they had to do something. After squabbling among themselves, tribal leaders finally elected a successor. They chose Abū Bakr. At the age of fifty-nine, this stooped thin man with a dyed red beard was the overwhelming best choice. Had he not been close to the Prophet during the rise of Islam? And was he not the father-in-law of Muhammad? Moreover, was he not also the man the Prophet himself had picked to be the official prayer leader in the mosque in Mecca? In addition, Abū Bakr enjoyed a wide reputation as a wise, gentle, and religious man.

"There can be little doubt that if Muhammad was the mind and imagination of primitive Islam," writes H. G. Wells, "Abu Bekr [Bakr] was its conscience and its will. Throughout their life together it was Muhammad who said the thing, but it was Abu Bekr who believed the thing. When Muhammad wavered, Abu Bekr sustained him."[42]

Nobody expected Abū Bakr to be another Muhammad, however. Instead, Muslim leaders appointed him to serve as caliph, or deputy of the Muslims. Scarcely had Abū Bakr settled into his new role when he had to face up a huge and disturbing problem: the possible extinction of Islam.

Upon hearing of Muhammad's death, many desert tribes that earlier had succumbed to the Muslims were now cutting their links with Mecca. Since Muhammad was dead, they argued, their obligations to abide by Muslim rule were canceled. Specifically, they refused to pay any more money to Muslim tax collectors.

Infuriated by this breakaway movement, known as the Apostasy, or Ridda in Arabic, and to keep Islam from showing any signs of unraveling, Abū Bakr ordered an army composed heavily of Bedouins to squash revolts throughout the Arabian peninsula. Under the command of a fabled warrior named Khālid ibn al-Walīd, Muslims went to war and easily stamped out the Apostasy by 632.

In an earlier time Khālid had fought against Muslims. But now he was a Muslim convert and such an ardent champion of Islam that before his death Muhammad designated him the Sword of Islam.

Emboldened by military success, this sword-swinging convert was not satisfied with suppressing the Apostasy. Next he led his Bedouin warriors on raids beyond the Arabian borders into Persia and Syria.

Greatly motivated by desire for booty, these raiders set the stage for even larger invasions that changed the world forever.

Muslims Defeat Two Empires

Although Muslims triumphed over Arabia, their peninsula was overshadowed by two great empires that lay to the north. These two massive forces had long rivaled each other for power and control of Mediterranean and Middle Eastern lands. Headquartered in Constantinople, today known as Istanbul, Turkey, the Byzantine Empire was an Orthodox Christian power that represented the eastern half of the old Roman Empire.

Its potent enemy, the Persian Empire, which lay to its east, had at its core Zoroas-trianism—a monotheistic religion containing some elements of Judaism and Islam.

After Abū Bakr died in 634, both Byzantium and Persia found themselves suddenly under attack from the Muslim Arabs. Urging the Muslim raiders ever onward was Islam's third caliph, 'Umar ibn al-Khattāb, whom Abū Bakr named his successor shortly before he died. Bald, towering, and broad shouldered, 'Umar was a pious and robust caliph with a fiery temper and a fast whip, which he frequently used against his men for violations of Koranic rule. He is said to have ordered the flogging of his own son. 'Umar, however, was also guided by an unswerving sense of justice. When, according to legend, he learned that he had unjustly whipped a Bedouin, he demanded that the man whip him the same number of strokes to even the score.

'Umar and his followers relentlessly pursued the jihad in their quest to spread the Islamic creed. They often wreaked havoc on the lands they conquered.

During the early days of his leadership, 'Umar called himself the Successor of the Successor of the Messenger of God. Later he simplified his title to Commander of the Faithful, a term also used by many future caliphs.

Under 'Umar Islam began a period of bold expansion and conquest. Between 636 and 651 besieged lands from the Middle East to northern Africa fell into Muslim hands one by one: Syria, Iraq, Mesopotamia, Egypt, Iran, and Morocco.

A harsh, strict, and uncompromising devotee of Muhammad, 'Umar had little use for any non-Islamic ideas. When Muslim warriors captured Alexandria, for example, they wantonly destroyed a fabled library that held priceless academic works of the ancient past. Though scholars disagree over 'Umar's personal participation in this destructive act, historian Edward Gibbon does report the caliph as saying: "If these writings of the Greeks agree with the word of God [Allah], they are useless and need not be preserved; if they disagree, they are pernicious [wicked] and ought to be destroyed."[43]

Muslim Victory over the Mighty

How had a medley of primitive desert tribes wrested power, control, and property from two of the world's mightiest empires? For one thing, the Byzantines and Persians were exhausted by war with each other and thus vulnerable to Arab attacks.

In contrast to the mighty Persians and Byzantines, the invading Arabs appeared poorly armed and undermanned. Nonetheless, they enjoyed certain intangible advantages. Buoyed by their military success in quelling revolts in Arabia, they plunged into battle in an aggressive fighting mood. Religious passion also spurred them into action. They were convinced that the Koran compelled them to spread Islam to all nonbelievers.

"Surely the major determinant of Arab success," argues historian William McNeill, "was the discipline and courage inspired in the rank and file by the certainty, confirmed with each victory, that Allah was indeed fighting on their side."[44]

A compelling nonreligious reason also motivated desert-dwelling Bedouins to wage war. Making raids for glory and booty was a time-honored tradition. Thus, when the drought-stricken Bedouins found themselves enticed by rich and fertile lands that lay beyond their own barren deserts, they poured into the north, eager to carry out 'Umar's commands.

"The predominant incentives that drove the Bedouin out of the peninsula were bodily hunger and greed . . . [and] the endless opportunities for enrichment offered by the cultivated societies they overran," writes Joel Carmichael.[45]

Jihad: Holy War

The invading Muslims often justified their warlike actions by claiming that they were carrying out a jihad, or holy war. Like much of Islam, this term is often misunderstood in the West. At times Muslims do invoke the concept of jihad to wage war, if done for religious purpose. "Fight in the cause of Allah against those who fight against you," implores the Koran.[46]

But *jihad* also evokes another meaning to Muslims: the idea of struggling to lead a virtuous life and to overcome societal problems through teaching and preaching in accordance with Koranic principles:

Muslim Rules of Engagement

In The Age of Faith *Will Durant quotes Abū Bakr as he clarifies these rules of conflict that his Muslim warriors must obey.*

"Be just . . . be valiant; die rather than yield; be merciful; slay neither old men, nor women, nor children. Destroy no fruit trees, grain, or cattle. Keep your word, even to your enemies. Molest not those religious persons who live retired from the world, but compel the rest of mankind to become Moslems or pay us tribute. If they refuse these terms, slay them."

Khālid's Rules of Surrender

In 635 Khālid ibn al-Walīd made these demands of a defeated enemy. Quoted in Desmond Stewart's Early Islam, *they became the standard terms of surrender for those defeated by Muslims.*

"In the name of Allah, the compassionate, the merciful, this is what Khalid ibn Al-Walid would grant to the inhabitants of Damascus.

. . . He promises to give them security for their lives, property and churches. Their city wall shall not be demolished, neither shall any Muslim be quartered in their houses. Thereunto we give to them the pact of Allah and the protection of His Prophet, the Caliphs and the believers. So long as they pay the tax, nothing but good shall befall them."

"Strive in the cause of Allah a perfect striving, for He has exalted you and has laid no hardship upon you in the matter of religion."[47]

Under 'Umar and many of the caliphs who followed him, jihad often provided the reason for holy war against non-Muslims. Two worlds existed at this time in the minds of early Muslims. All the peoples and lands under Muslim control were considered Dar al-Islam, or Realm of Islam. Those still beyond Muslim reach were Dar al-Harb, or Realm of War.

Historian Dilip Hiro writes:

The sustained expansion of the Dar al-Islam through the waging of jihad, holy war, helped 'Umar to hold together the coalition of Arabian tribes under his leadership. He combined the expansionist drive with a well-designed plan to maintain a large standing army and inculcate [implant] it with Islamic teachings and practices.[48]

'Umar was a true believer. His use of military power was for the sole purpose of spreading what he unquestioningly held to be the word of God. Unlike many Muslim leaders who came after him, he did not appear to seek personal glory, wealth, or fame. In fact, he recoiled from such trappings and deliberately lived in poverty.

Nor was he pleased with possessing great power. Instead, his role as a mighty leader seems to have confused and distressed him. "By God! I know not whether I am Caliph or Emperor," 'Umar once cried. "And if I am Emperor, it is a fearful thing."[49]

Fearful or not, the great and unfolding power of Muslim's caliphs changed the face of the earth.

Chapter

4 The Splintering of Islam

How the conquered peoples living in Persian and Byzantine lands behaved during the Muslim attacks often determined how Muslims treated them. If the captives yielded peacefully, then Muslims generally allowed them to keep their lands and pay a tax to their new rulers for protection. Those who resisted the Muslim forces, however, often saw their lands confiscated and divided among the newcomers.

Benefits of Muslim Life

Converts to Islam realized an immediate benefit: as Muslims, they paid a much lower tax to the new regime. In theory they were also supposed to be treated as equals to Arab Muslims, though this seldom happened right away. During Islam's early years Muslims considered Islam a religion for Arabs only. Thus, Arabs were not eager to share the wealth and booty of victory with non-Arabs. Under 'Umar's rule, in fact, Muslim soldiers were forbidden to colonize any conquered territory. Instead, they lived outside the towns and villages in military garrisons where they spent their off-duty time practicing Islam.

In time the captured populations were integrated into the Muslim fold. A newly converted non-Arab, however, had to be sponsored or adopted by an Arab tribe. Even when this did occur, non-Arab Muslims were known as *mawalis*, or clients, to identify them as being different from the Arabs.

Converts and nonbelievers alike soon discovered they were usually less oppressed by their new Arab rulers than they had been under Byzantine or Persian rule. As one Syrian explained to a newly arrived Muslim warrior: "We like your rule and justice far better than the state of oppression and tyranny under which we have been living."[50]

Jews, Christians, and Zoroastrians made up a class that received special status. Islam acknowledges that God also revealed himself through Scriptures to Jews and Christians. They were the People of the Book or *dhimmis*. When Muslims captured Jerusalem in 638, for instance, 'Umar promised local Christian leaders, "Verily, you are assured of the complete security of your lives, and your churches, which will not be inhabited nor destroyed by the Muslims."[51]

By paying a special tax, or *jizya*, the People of the Book could practice their own religions without punishment from Muslims. However, they often had to wear special clothes to signify their religion and were not allowed to carry weapons.

Islamic law also prohibited the *dhimmis* from participating in certain activities such as the building of new churches or synagogues.

Generally Muslims allowed the conquered peoples to practice their own religions under either Byzantines or Persians and enjoy far greater freedoms than they had before.

The Death of 'Umar

In 644 Islam was pitched into another crisis of leadership when a Christian slave assassinated 'Umar while he led Muslim prayers. The man who served as Islam's puritanical and militant leader died in a patched shirt and cloak.

Unlike Abū Bakr, 'Umar had not chosen a successor before his death. Instead, he had created a council to make this important decision. This group now made its choice: an old and weak aristocrat named 'Uthmān ibn 'Affān. Tribal leaders may have picked 'Uthmān because they believed he would be easy to manipulate behind the scenes.

One thing was certain: the selection of 'Uthmān was controversial. He was a member of the Umayyad clan that had once been an enemy of Muhammad, a fact well remembered by Islam's founding members, many of whom were companions of Muhammad. They suspected that the Umayyads were mere opportunists who had converted to Islam for political reasons.

Their fears intensified when the new caliph gave all the desirable government positions to his own relatives regardless of their qualifications. Such overt favoritism outraged many Muslims.

'Uthmān's opponents also seethed over the way the new government collected and distributed the vast amounts of wealth coming from the occupied countries. Under a system begun earlier by 'Umar, all tribute and booty was turned over to the ever growing ruling class in Medina. 'Umar, however, had at least expressed misgivings about the corruptive force of too much wealth. Once he allegedly wept at the sight of Persian wealth that fell to Muslim hands and cried aloud, "I fear all this wealth and luxury will in the end ruin my people."[52] The new regime showed no such qualms.

Growing Problems

Tensions worsened in 654 when a Muslim prophet in Egypt began to whip angry crowds into fury by preaching that 'Uthmān was a godless man with no legitimate authority to rule. He also proclaimed that Muhammad would come back to life. The only true successor, insisted the prophet, was 'Alī, a relative of the Prophet and a leader of Muhammad's clan.

In June 656 five hundred angry Muslim warriors, led by Muhammad ibn Abū Bakr—the son of Islam's first caliph—traveled from Egypt to Medina to demand 'Uthmān's resignation. The aged ruler heard their complaints but warned them, "I will not abdicate. How can I throw off the mantle which God has placed about my shoulders?"[53]

Later 'Uthmān publicly condemned the men which infuriated them. One night they burst into 'Uthmān's residence and killed the eighty-three-year-old caliph.

As word of the assassination quickly spread, other Umayyad leaders raced away from the city in fear.

The episode marked a disturbing milestone in the history of Islam, for it was the first time Muslims had killed a Muslim caliph. With 'Uthmān's death, Islam sank into a dark period of bickering, intrigue, and vicious competition for power.

Rivals Fracture Islam

'Alī was a bald, stocky man of fifty-five with a white beard and a strong reputation as a generous, capable soldier and gifted speaker. His family ties to the Prophet were strong. He was Muhammad's nephew, adopted son, and the husband of Fātimah, Muhammad's only living child.

'Alī and his supporters unswervingly believed that only a family member of Muhammad had the right to be caliph. They also maintained that, contrary to what others believed, Muhammad had selected 'Alī to be his successor. The first three caliphs, they insisted, were interlopers. In time, Muslims favoring this view evolved into a distinct, separate branch of Islam called Shia, or *shiat-u-'Alī* (party of 'Alī).

In contrast, those who accepted the authority of Umayyad caliphs became known as the Sunni, or orthodox, Muslims. The division between the Sunni and Shia forever bisected Islam.

One of 'Alī's fiercest opponents was Aishah—Abū Bakr's daughter and a favored wife of Muhammad—who was jealous of Fātimah, daughter of Muhammad and Khadījah, and who coveted the leadership of Islam for herself. Aishah may have nursed a grudge against 'Alī that dated back several years to when she felt herself wrongfully accused by him of unfaithfulness to Muhammad.

For whatever reason, she ordered her troops to prepare an attack on 'Alī to depose him. She was joined in battle by two other powerful leaders: Zobeir and Talha. These conspirators' excuse for waging war was that 'Alī had not vigorously prosecuted 'Uthmān's murderers. A message from Mu'āwiyah, the governor of Syria, expressed what many Muslims were thinking: "I have seen sixty thousand men at the mosque at Damascus, weeping at the sight of 'Uthmān's bloody shirt and cursing the murderers!"[54]

'Alī had no choice but to defend his rule with force. With nine hundred armed men, including the real ringleader of 'Uthmān's death, Muhammad ibn Abū Bakr, 'Alī headed to southern Iraq to meet his foes. There his men defeated the challengers in a bloody encounter that became known as the Battle of the Camel to commemorate Aishah's Bedouin-styled command of her troops from the back of a camel.

This military clash was the first time one Muslim army fought another. In the centuries to come Islam would see more such conflicts. The unity of the *umma* was shattered forever.

Mu'āwiyah's Challenge

'Alī now moved the headquarters of Muslim power from Medina to al-Kufa, Iraq. By doing this, he hoped to repay the residents of al-Kufa, who had aided him in

A formidable military opponent, 'Alī meets his foes head on in battle. Beset by troubles, 'Alī's rule ended with his assassination in 661.

battle. The move also made logistical sense; al-Kufa was a more centrally located spot for a Muslim capital in the vast and growing empire. This change, however, diminished Arabia in significance as a power center.

'Alī's troubles, however, were far from over. His reign continued to be haunted by the memory of 'Uthmān's murder. Soon another foe—Mu'āwiyah, the Umayyad governor of Syria and son of Muhammad's old enemy, Abū Sufyan—schemed to bring 'Alī down. In Damascus Mu'āwiyah appeared before a large crowd to denounce 'Alī and sent them into a frenzy when he produced 'Uthmān's bloody clothes and the fingers severed from the hand of 'Uthmān's widow, Nailah, as she tried to protect her husband from his killers. Mu'āwiyah publicly demanded that 'Alī produce 'Uthmān's killer and punish him. Mu'āwiyah may also have wanted to restore the power of the Quraysh elite, who had seen their influence downgraded through the years by the rise of Muhammad and his followers.

When 'Alī failed to produce 'Uthmān's assassins, Mu'āwiyah raised a military force in Damascus and attacked 'Alī's army in 657 at Siffin in Syria. The fighting, however, went badly for Mu'āwiyah. Most likely his armies would have been annihilated if not for the power of a single brilliant idea. Amr, who was one of Mu'āwiyah's military leaders, ordered his men to tie copies of the Koran to their spear tips and cry "Let God decide" as they rushed into battle.

The stunt worked. 'Alī's men were so stunned and intimidated by the sea of pages from their holy book that they refused to fight and insisted that 'Alī negotiate a settlement with Mu'āwiyah.

Under pressure, 'Alī let Mu'āwiyah and his men return to their homes while arbitrators from both sides spent the next six months pondering a decision.

This move satisfied many of 'Alī's soldiers, but it infuriated others, who thought he had undermined the will of God by allowing arbitrators to decide the outcome of a holy war. Many of 'Alī's men were also angry that Mu'āwiyah's warriors had been spared. By the thousands these disillusioned soldiers broke away from 'Alī's army and formed their own fighting force—the Kharijjites, or seceders.

New Religious Concepts

These breakaway warriors also developed their own religious concepts. The caliph, they argued, should be elected and subject to removal from office by all Muslims. The Kharijjites also demanded an end to what they saw as excessive privilege and luxury enjoyed by the Muslim ruling classes.

When 'Alī failed to convince the Kharijjites to return, he felt he had no choice except to subdue them with those troops still loyal to him. Though victorious, the caliph found himself weakened militarily and more vulnerable than ever.

At last the arbitrators made their decision. Both 'Alī and Mu'āwiyah, they announced, should renounce their claims as caliphs. Instead, Muslims should elect a leader.

Immediately Mu'āwiyah defied the decision and declared himself caliph anyway.

A Father's Warning

As quoted in Robert Payne's History of Islam, *Mu'āwiyah, while he lay dying, warned his son Yazid of these perils:*

"The restless people of Iraq will encourage Husayn to attempt the empire. Defeat him, but afterward deal gently with him, for truly the blood of the Messenger of God runs through his veins. It is Abdallah ibn [az]-Zubayr I fear most. He is fierce as a lion and crafty as a fox, and must be destroyed root and branch!"

And soon it became clear that the arbitrators had wasted their time. On the morning of January 24, 661, 'Alī heard a gaggle of geese honking. When a servant tried to disperse them, 'Alī said "Let them cry. They are weeping for my funeral."[55] His words were prophetic. A while later a Kharijjite rammed a poisoned sword into 'Alī's skull and killed him.

Mu'āwiyah was now unopposed. When 'Alī's son, Hasan, considered succeeding his slain father, Mu'āwiyah cowed the younger man with a threat of attack and bought him off with a generous pension for life.

Now the undisputed leader of Islam, Mu'āwiyah moved the caliphate to Damascus in Syria and set up the Umayyad dynasty. He felt triumphant and vindicated. The son of Abū Sufyan had finally defeated the followers of Muhammad. Once again the Quraysh family was in a position of power. But now they ruled on a scale never before imagined: this time they commanded a vast and growing empire.

When Mu'āwiyah moved the caliphate from a desert oasis to the cosmopolitan city of Damascus, he created a major change for Islam. During Umayyad expansion, Damascus grew in power and influence. With each Muslim conquest, more and more booty and taxes poured into the official coffers.

A Distinctive Culture Takes Shape

Although the Umayyads borrowed Byzantine governmental institutions to fit their needs, they promoted Arabic as the official language across the empire. Islamic money was minted and replaced Byzantine and Persian currencies. The Umayyads also established efficient communication and transportation systems and undertook massive public works building projects. All the while, an Arabic military class became the ruling caste. "Under the Umayyads, a dis-

Sufi Self-Discipline

The importance of self-discipline in the life of the Sufi Hatim al-Asamm is expressed in this passage from The Word of Islam, *edited by John Alden Williams.*

"Hatim al-Asamm was asked, 'On what do you base your trust of God?' He replied, 'On four principles. I learned that no-one can eat my daily bread except me, and I calmed my Self with this knowledge. I learned that no-one performs my acts but me, and so I busy myself with them. I learned that Death will come suddenly, and so I run to meet him; and I learned that I am never hidden from God's sight wherever I am, so I behave modestly before Him.'"

tinctive Islamic culture began to take form, influenced largely by their Arab background," Desmond Stewart points out.[56]

What kind of leader was Mu'āwiyah? "Handsome, elegant and suave, delighting in luxury and power, amused by his own behavior and capable of surprising acts of toleration, outwardly warm but possessed of an inner core of cold steel, he [Mu'āwiyah] was in every way the opposite of Muhammad . . . ," writes Robert Payne.[57]

For the most part, Muslims enjoyed a period of peace and prosperity under Mu'āwiyah's competent and kinglike rule. He feared that upon his death, however, the Islamic world would once again be cast into turmoil if another controversial election of a caliph was held. Therefore, he proclaimed that the power of the caliph would be passed onto his next-oldest male relative when he died.

Thus, when Mu'āwiyah died in 680, his son Yazīd took power. But trouble over leadership flared immediately despite Mu'āwiyah's best intentions. A group of Shia, or Shiites, in al-Kufa decided to oppose Yazīd and notified Husayn, another son of 'Alī, that they would support him as the rightful caliph. Husayn accepted their offer and with seventy followers departed Mecca and headed for al-Kufa.

Yazīd learned of the plot to oust him and took action to stop it. When Husayn's caravan was about twenty-five miles outside of al-Kufa, Yazīd's men suddenly appeared and attacked. They slaughtered all males in the party and cut off Husayn's head. One of Yazīd's officers, however, complained when one of the leaders rolled the head over with a stick: "Gently, he was the grandson of the Prophet. By Allah, I have seen those lips kissed by the blessed mouth of Mohammed."[58]

These killings deeply traumatized the Shiites. Husayn's murder compounded the sense of outrage and injustice they already felt over the murder of 'Alī. Today Shiites still commemorate the lives of 'Alī, Hasan, and Husayn with an annual passion play.

Next Yazīd's troops faced another revolt at Mecca led by 'Abd Allāh ibn az-Zubayr, a grandson of Abū Bakr and fierce hater of the Umayyads. Here the fighting was so destructive that the sacred black stone shattered when hit by rocks from catapults and the Kaaba burned to the ground.

Not until 'Abd al-Malik, a relative of Mu'āwiyah, took power in 685 did the chaos within Islam begin to subside. Force was al-Malik's solution for holding the empire together. Years later his deathbed advice to his son Walīd in 705 was "Why are you mourning? When I am dead, put on your leopard-skin, gird yourself with your sword, and cut off the head of everyone who gets in your way."[59]

"During the ensuing peace, " writes Will Durant, "Abd-al-Malik wrote poetry, patronized letters, attended to eight wives, and reared fifteen sons. . . . His reign of twenty years paved the way for the accomplishments of his son Walid (705–15) . . . . The march of Arab conquest was now resumed."[60]

Umayyad Victories

Under Umayyad command Arab armies moved into present-day Morocco, Algeria, and Tunisia in North Africa. Here they mingled with a nomadic people called the Berbers and converted them to Islam.

In 711, groups of Muslim Berbers (pictured) pushed into and conquered Spain and Portugal.

In 711 a force of Muslim Berbers crossed the Strait of Gibraltar, moved into the Iberian peninsula, and began a long campaign of conquest. Within a decade they drove out another group of invaders—the Visigoths—and took control of Spain and Portugal.

The Muslims pushed on heading for the heartland of Europe. They were stopped in the Pyrenees by troops under the command of Frankish leader Charles Martel at the Battle of Tours in 732. To Europeans this Muslim loss was momentous. Had Martel failed to blunt the Muslim drive, all Europe might have fallen to Islam conquerors.

But the Muslims still had Spain. Here Islamic culture took root and flourished for over seven hundred years. Its influences are still evident today from architecture to literature.

By 751 Umayyad forces had spread Islam all the way to the Indus River valley in India and into central China. As Islam expanded in other lands, it absorbed millions of people of many races and faiths from Africa to Asia. Generally friction between these various multitudes did not rise to the surface enough to cause serious disturbance as long as the excitement of conquest enthralled and distracted the Muslims.

As successful as they were, however, Muslim warriors failed during this period of renewed expansion to conquer an important and long-coveted prize: Constantinople, a major Christian stronghold and a gateway to Asia and Europe.

Opposition to the Umayyads

As the dynamic of expansion began to wither in 718 after Muslim forces failed to conquer Constantinople, internal problems emerged and shook the foundations of the empire. Political rivalry topped the list of troubles. Muslim leaders in Persia, Egypt, and Arabia deeply resented the power held by the Umayyads in Damascus, Syria. They wanted greater authority for themselves and bickered endlessly. Many Muslims resented the wealthy Umayyad rulers and the privileges enjoyed by the military elite in Damascus. Also, many non-Arabs in the conquered areas resented their treatment as second-class citizens by the Umayyads.

Until they were defeated by Charles Martel at the decisive Battle of Tours (pictured), Muslims posed a serious threat to western Europe.

Muslim troops were also growing restless, Many of them continued to live segregated from those they had conquered in special garrison cities outside the main urban areas of the empire. More and more they began to resent the gulf between their own spartan lives and those of the superiors who lived in luxury in Damascus.

Ironically, many Arabs by now had lost interest in converting their captives to Islam. Since converts were exempt from the special tax put on nonbelievers, Muslim leaders worried that conversions were costing the empire much needed tax revenues.

Religious Disputes

Finally, Islam under Umayyad rule was also plagued by never ending religious arguments among Muslim factions. One of them—the Sufi—called for renunciation of the Umayyad's military elite's soft living and urged a return to the severe example set by Muhammad. The Sufis' adherence to mystical beliefs also set them apart from most Muslims.

Meanwhile, the Kharijjites developed into a revolutionary, puritanical cult that demanded a holy war against the Umayyad rulers. Many Kharijjites believed that the Koran obliged them to see all human acts as either permitted or forbidden. In their eyes, anybody who did not conform to their orthodox views was considered a sinner and a traitor against the *umma*. Punishment was excommunication or execution for anyone who refused to repent.

Adding to the atmosphere of unrest mounting across the empire were the Shi-

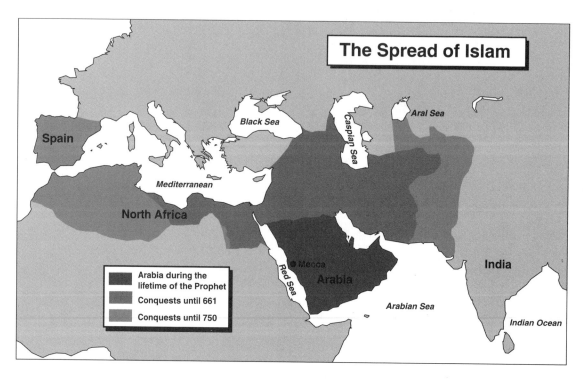

The Spread of Islam

Spain

Black Sea

Aral Sea

Caspian Sea

Mediterranean

North Africa

India

Red Sea

Mecca

Arabia

Arabian Sea

Indian Ocean

Arabia during the lifetime of the Prophet

Conquests until 661

Conquests until 750

Why a Great Power Fell

As quoted in Robert Payne's History of Islam, *a high-ranking official in the Umyyad government named Abdullah gives his Abbasid captors this explanation for the collapse of Umyyad power.*

"These were our faults—we gave to pleasure the time we should have devoted to government. We laid heavy burdens on our people, and so alienated them from our rule. We taxed them so heavily, and gave them so little opportunity for redress [compensation] that they prayed for deliverance from us. We left our fields uncultivated, and our treasury was empty. We trusted our ministers, but they pursued their own selfish interests and governed the country in their own right and left us in ignorance. The pay of the army was always in arrears, and so in the hour of danger they sided with the enemy; and our allies failed us when we needed them most. But the chief causes of the fall of our empire lay in our ignorance in government and our innocence, for we never knew what was happening."

ites, who still fumed with hatred for the Umayyads. This group insisted that their imam was a divinely inspired descendant of the Prophet who deserved to be the caliph.

There was also a branch of the Shiites named the Fatimads, who believed that only descendants of Muhammad's daughter, Fātimah, held the divine authority to rule.

When Umayyad leaders in Damascus realized their empire was becoming increasingly hard to govern, they divided it into five regions, each with its own governor. Eventually, though, these governors became so powerful that they scorned the authority of Damascus and attempted to rule independently.

As the various groups and factions smoldered with anger, envy, resentment, and pious certainty, one Muslim tribe steeled itself for an attempt to take over the Muslim Empire.

The Abbasid Revolt

In 747 a Meccan clan, the Abbasids, shook the Muslim world with revolt. They were led by Abū al-'Abbās, a ruthless Meccan who claimed his ancestry to an uncle of Muhammad. But the real strength of the revolt came from Persian Muslims in eastern Iran. Here many Persians considered themselves culturally superior to the Arabs who had conquered them. They had long resented the way the Umayyads treated them as second-class citizens and wanted revenge.

Using a black banner as a symbol of revolt, the Abbasids toppled the Umayyads and installed a new caliph: Abū al-'Abbās, who now called himself the Bloodthirsty, or as-Saffāh. Taking no chances that the Umayyads would regain their power, al-'Abbās ordered his men to hunt down and kill all Umayyad princes everywhere in the empire. The warriors carried out their mission with chilling efficiency. Author Will Durant describes how one of the caliph's subordinates, a Syrian governor named 'Abd Allāh, obeyed his instructions:

> He announced an amnesty to the Umayyads, and to confirm it he invited eighty of their leaders to dinner. While they ate, his hidden soldiers, at his signal, put them all to the sword. Carpets were spread over the fallen men, and the feast was resumed by the Abbasid diners over the bodies of their foes, and to the music of dying groans. The corpses of several Umayyad caliphs were exhumed, the almost fleshless skeletons were scourged [whipped], hanged, and burned, and the ashes were scattered to the winds. [61]

During this frenzy of ghoulishness, Abbasid soldiers failed to kill one important member of the Umayyad family: Prince 'Abd ar-Rahmān. Chased by Abbasids, he managed to swim across the Euphrates River and make his way to the Iberian Peninsula. Here he formed an army of supporters and reigned over all Iberia.

By 754 the Umayyads were destroyed. Although the Abbasids now controlled the Muslim Empire, they had done so by force, not through claims of hereditary right or election. Thus, they were forced to develop a new explanation to legitimize their authority. Borrowing the pomp and ceremony common to Persian royalty, Islam's new rulers claimed that their right to govern came from heaven. The caliph now called his rule the Shadow of God on Earth.

Life Under the Abbasids

Abbasid officials acted fast to win over a skeptical populace. They declared equality for all Muslims, Arabs, and non-Arabs alike. As a result, the gulf between the garrison-bound Arab Muslims and non-Arabs broke down. Soon intermingling took place among the different races and ethnic groups throughout the empire. Consequently, Arabs began to lose their tribal identities and Bedouin values. The Abbasids also won the support of many non-Arabs by including them in the new government.

Unlike their predecessors, the Abassids aligned themselves not with luxury-minded city or military classes, but with a religious class—the ulema, the scholars of Islam.

There was a notable exception, however: the Abbasid caliphs adopted courtly mannerisms that set them apart from the masses of everyday Muslims. Like the ancient Persian kings before them, they lived in great splendor, pomp, and ceremony, with many servants attending them, seldom seen by the public. Inside his palace an Abbasid ruler hid himself behind a curtain to create a mood of unapproachable mystery and wonder. Anyone wishing to talk to him first had to lie prostrate and kiss the floor. Nearby, a concealed executioner stood ready to behead the visitor if commanded.

This display of power disturbed many Muslims. In contrast, Muhammad had lived simply and in daily contact with other Muslims. And why not? Was not the *umma* a community of equals?

Eventually the Abbasid caliphate became so removed from the everyday affairs of the empire that it ceased to rule at all. Instead, caliphs turned over the power of running the government to an appointed individual, the vizier, who became the second most powerful man in the empire.

Patrons of the Arts

The state of balance of daily life, a smooth-functioning government, and the enormous wealth pouring in from the empire, however, enabled the Abbasids to become patrons of the arts. In fact, writes author Desmond Stewart, during the early centuries of Abbasid rule, "Islam was to reach its pinnacle—a brief period when it was the greatest force on earth, and its capital the fairest and foremost city in the world."[62]

Chapter

5 The Abbasid Golden Age

By means of military conquest, Muslims spread their religion across the Middle East into Africa, Europe, and Asia, where they encountered many new races and societies. Jews, Greeks, Syrians, Christians, Persians, Indians, Berbers, Africans, Russians, and many other nationalities and ethnic groups contributed to a new and growing multiethnic culture that reached a golden age under the Abbasids.

Underneath this quiltwork of cultures, however, were the foundations of Islam. A Muslim who traveled in the vast Islamic world, whether it was Spain, North Africa, or northwest India, had much in common with the local population. The Arabic language and the basic principles of Islam gave all Muslims an underlying unity and outlook on the world.

What also held this vast empire together and provided the economic basis for a new world power was a well-developed system of trade.

Trade

Trade and commerce had been highly respected for centuries in the Arab world. And because Muhammad had been a merchant, Muslims gave businesspeople a higher status than they might have enjoyed in some other cultures.

Under the Abbasids no trade barriers existed throughout the empire. To facilitate international commerce even more, Muslims developed sophisticated banking systems. Receipts, checks, and letters of credit were all commonly found throughout the Muslim world. Muslims also developed trade associations and joint-stock companies in which people pooled their money to start a business. By ships or by camel caravans, Muslim trade took place from Spain across the Middle East to India, Ceylon, and into Russia, China, and the islands of the South Seas.

The Splendor of Baghdad

The early Abbasid rulers moved the Muslim capital from Damascus to the banks of the Tigris River in Iraq, where they ordered the building of Baghdad—the Round City—which became a political, economic, cultural, and to a lesser degree, religious, center. Three concentric round walls protected the magnificent city. At the core of the innermost wall was the Green Dome of the caliph's palace, which served as the focal point for the entire urban

An Arabian market. Muslims encouraged and facilitated trade and commerce, which flourished across the huge empire.

area. Here from 786 to 809 ruled Hārūn ar-Rashīd, whose life became the inspiration for many of the tales in the book, *A Thousand and One Nights*, a world literary masterpiece.

Historian Philip Hitti offers this description:

> History and legend have conspired to make the court of Harun al-Rashid and his son al-Maum the most glamorous one in Islam. In the midst of the old city and covering about a third of its area stood the royal palaces. . . . Especially on festivals, weddings, receptions for foreign envoys and other ceremonial occasions did the courtly wealth and splendor make their full display. The princely [generosity] . . . of Harun . . . and his immediate successors attracted musicians, singers, dancers, wits and poets from all over the realm.[63]

Located at the crossroads of major trade routes from faraway lands, Baghdad quickly became the empire's center of culture, arts, and new ideas. Cargo-laden ships even sailed from the Persian Gulf to make way along the Tigris to unload exotic merchandise on the docks of Baghdad. In busy, noisy bazaars merchants enticed shoppers with delicate porcelain items and colorful silks from China, spices and rubies from India, and swords, honey, and wax from Russia. Oranges and the art of papermaking arrived from China. Merchants hawked perfumes, silk, and cotton, along with bronze and wood crafts, carpets and textiles, exquisite glass items, pottery, glazed tile, and metal crafts—all originating from far-flung areas of the empire.

People were also for sale in the bazaars. At slave markets slaves, both black and white, seized in Africa and Scandinavia, were auctioned off to work as household servants.

A High Standard of Living

Thanks to sustained prosperity and a cosmopolitan way of life, Baghdad and several other leading Muslim cities offered Muslims a standard of living that far surpassed that found in the rude, muddy villages of Christian Europe at the time. Well-planned Muslim cities boasted beau-

Choosing the Site of Baghdad

This excerpt from Albert Hourani's History of the Arab Peoples *contains ninth-century Muslim historian al-Tabarī's description of a visit by Abbasid ruler al-Mansūr to the future site of Islam's new capital, Baghdad.*

"He came to the area of the bridge and crossed at the present site of Qasr al-Salam. He then prayed the afternoon prayer. It was in summer, and at the site of the palace there was then a priest's church. He spent the night there, and awoke next morning having passed the sweetest and gentlest night on earth. He stayed, and everything he saw pleased him. Then he said, 'This is the site on which I shall build. Things can arrive here by way of the Euphrates, Tigris, and a network of canals. Only a place like this will support the army and the general populace.' So he laid it out and assigned monies for its construction, and laid the first brick with his own hand, saying, 'In the name of God, and praise to Him. The earth is God's; He causes to inherit of it whom He wills among His servants, and the result thereof is to them that fear Him.' Then he said, 'Build, and God bless you!'"

tiful fountains, public baths, running water, good restaurants, and public libraries. New labor-saving innovations such as ovens, frying pans, and porcelain dishes made life easier in Muslim towns and settlements.

The Abbasid government operated a postal system and a judicial system, kept up roads and bridges, maintained medical clinics and mosques, and provided for the defense of the people.

The Pilgrimage to Mecca

Though Baghdad was the cultural center of Islam, Mecca remained the empire's religious heart. Since Islam required all be-

lievers to make a pilgrimage to Mecca, this ancient city experienced a constant flow of foreigners from much of the world. Muslims of all ages came on foot or atop camels, horses, or donkeys. Some pilgrims braved turbulent seas and crossed vast stretches of parched land to make the hajj. Sometimes their journeys took years.

This international mixing, with its emphasis on brotherhood and equality, gave believers a powerful feeling of purpose and community. It also promoted a spirit of tolerance for peoples of other lands. But it produced a quite unexpected benefit: the constant mixing of peoples from faraway lands resulted in a lively exchange of new ideas, methods, foods, experiences, and inventions that enabled Islam to make great advancements in the arts and sciences.

Farming Advancements

In Baghdad the Abbasids focused a great deal of attention on cultivating the fertile lands located between the Tigris and Euphrates Rivers. They had two important reasons for doing this: to feed their growing population, and to improve property values to raise land taxes. Similar attempts to raise revenues for the government were made in other agricultural areas elsewhere in the empire.

Despite the high premium put on agriculture by the Abbasid government, many Muslims looked down on farming as a lowly pursuit far beneath their dignity. At least it played no important role in the lives of those with a Bedouin heritage. Thus, much of the physical labor in the fields was done by the non-Muslim *dhimmis*. Generally Arabic Muslims took part in agriculture only as administrators or supervisors.

Muslim fields provided an abundance of crops: wheat, barley, rice, sesame, sugar-

Pilgrims prepare to travel to Mecca from a port at Algiers. Pilgrimage to Mecca brought believers together from across the empire, resulting in the exchange of new ideas and customs.

cane, cotton, and flax. Fruit trees bore dates, olives, oranges, lemons, pomegranates, and peaches. Cultivated gardens produced eggplants, watermelons, and cucumbers. Botanists learned how to graft fruit trees and to make new hybrid fruits and plants.

At the same time, agriculturists developed advanced methods of irrigation, crop rotation, and fertilization that helped to turn arid areas of the Middle East and North Africa into highly fertile areas.

Through their efforts at stock breeding, Muslims created some of the world's finest equine bloodlines—including Arabians and thoroughbreds, mixtures of Arabian stallions and English mares. They also raised purebred camels, goats, dogs, and even elephants.

Philosophy

Throughout history human inquiry often meets a chilly reception in societies dominated by religious thought. In the Abbasid period, especially during the ninth and fourteenth centuries, however, the pursuit of knowledge was not only tolerated but encouraged. It was the Abbasid government under Caliph al-Ma'mun from 813 to 833, for instance, that created the House of Wisdom in Baghdad—a center of learning that housed an observatory, a scientific academy, a public library, and a translation center in 830. Here, scholars busily translated new and old manuscripts from Persia, India, Syria, and many other lands and cultures. But the works that excited Arab minds the most were those from the ancient Greek thinkers— Aristotle, Euclid, Ptolemy, Archimedes,

Galen, and others—that had almost disappeared from use in western Europe.

According to many Greek philosophers the universe was not really as disorderly and confusing as it seemed on the surface. Instead, an underlying order governed by natural laws shaped and caused the great events and happenings of the natural world. And through the power of human reason, argued the ancient Greeks, this order could be understood. "We must clear our minds . . . from all causes that blind people to the truth—old custom, party, spirit, personal rivalry or passion, the desire for influence," wrote Muslim scholar Abū ar-Rayhān Muhammad ibn Ahmad al-Bīrūni.[64]

To the Arabic-speaking Persian scholar, Ibn Sīnā, nicknamed the Prince of Philosophers, knowledge radiated in the form of ideas from God to the human body where it created a thinking human soul. "The function of the human soul . . . is not to eat and drink," he wrote, "neither does it require luxury. . . ; rather its function is to wait for the revelation of truth."[65]

Early Arabic philosophy was confined to exploring the themes of Islamic beliefs. But Arabic scholars eventually became so influenced by the Greek approach that they strove to study as many different fields of knowledge as possible. They also attempted to fashion a new type of philosophy, *falsafah*, which combined the ideas of the Greek masters Plato and Aristotle with those of Islam.

Arabic scholars shied away from the translations of Greek drama and poetry because so many of these writings contained Greek religious and mythological ideas, which Islamic purists frowned upon. Instead, they used Greek ideas to explore

Arab scientists mix compounds in the market. The unswerving experimentation of Arab alchemists paved the way for the evolution of modern chemistry.

and excel in other areas, especially in the field of science.

The Sciences

For many centuries chemical dabblers had experimented with alchemy—a mystical form of experimentation the Arabs borrowed from Egypt. In the ancient world many educated people believed that all metals came from the same substance. In vain they sought through the centuries to find an elusive essence called the philosopher's stone, which could be used to change base metals into gold. "Blood, hair, excrement, and other materials were . . . [subjected to testing] to see if they contained this magic *al-iksir* or essence," observes historian Will Durant.[66]

Alchemists also searched for a special elixir, or cure-all, that could give eternal youth to anyone who drank it. Much time

and talent was wasted in these impossible pursuits. Nonetheless, thanks to the relentless experimentation of Arabs with powders, elements, and compounds, the pseudoscience of alchemy evolved into the reputable field of chemistry. In fact, many of the basic implements of a Muslim laboratory—flasks, beakers, vials—are still used today. Modern chemists also rely on various chemical names that originated with Arab alchemists, such as alcohol, alkali, soda, alembic, and syrup.

Another area of Muslim expertise was that of optics. For centuries many Muslim scholars had pondered a popular, but erroneous theory of vision. This theory held that sight took place because the human eye shot out invisible rays that struck objects and then bounced back to the eye.

But Persian physicist Alhazen came to a startling new conclusion during the tenth century when he correctly concluded that rays of light bounced off

THE ABBASID GOLDEN AGE ■ **65**

objects and then moved to the eye. This scientific breakthrough became the basis for modern optics.

Muslim Medical Thought

At the time of Muhammad Arabs possessed only a basic knowledge of medicine. But through the centuries of Islamic expansion, Muslim scholars learned from ancient thinkers in other lands and began to add new knowledge and insights.

The most imposing physician during Islam's golden age was ar-Rāzī, or Rhazes as he was known in Europe. A notable poet, physician, and scientist, he wrote more than two hundred books on a variety of serious subjects. A majority of them concerned medicine. His most important work was a vast medical encyclopedia that included knowledge gathered from Hindu, Persian, Greek, Syrian, and Arabic sources. This masterpiece influenced physicians far beyond Islam's borders for centuries.

Rhazes was also a master clinician. He precisely observed and described the symptoms of infectious diseases and also began the practice of using animal gut to suture wounds.

The philosopher Ibn Sīnā, better known in Europe as Avicenna, wrote 170 books on subjects ranging from philosophy to astronomy to medicine. His great work, however, was the *Canon of Medicine*, a remarkable five-volume encyclopedia that focused primarily on the correct identification of symptoms and listed how diseases were transmitted. So esteemed was this massive work that European medical schools used it as the principal textbook from the twelfth to the seventeenth century.

Muslim doctors made great strides in the field of medicine. Among other achievements, they learned how to cauterize wounds, a practice which saved many lives on the battlefield.

Despite their many successes, Muslim doctors made only modest advances in surgery. Here they were held back by their religion. Since Islam forbade them to cut open human cadavers or to use vivisection—the dissecting of living creatures—they had to learn anatomy by relying on Greek writings and by dissecting dead apes. Nonetheless, Muslim physicians developed several successful surgical techniques. In the tenth century, for example, they knew how to perform abdominal and cranial surgery. They amputated diseased arms and legs and cut away cancerous sections from healthy tissue. Cataracts on eyes were skillfully treated. Muslim doctors developed a way to vaccinate against smallpox. In Cordova, Spain, Islam's greatest surgeon, al-Zahrawi, learned to cauterize wounds and crush stones that appeared in the human bladder.

To spare their patients the pain of surgery, Muslim doctors created a variety of painkillers with ingredients that included opium, hashish, and wine. These narcotics, however, were but just a sampling of the many drugs produced by medieval Muslims.

Astronomy

As trade and religious fervor took Muslims farther into new and uncharted lands and seas, the need for travel aids increased dramatically. Eventually Muslim geographers produced some of the world's most extensive and accurate maps, atlases, calendars, charts, and guidebooks to assist the traveling Muslims.

Aiding them in their travels was a rediscovery of a nearly forgotten Greek invention: the astrolabe, a device that Muslims called the mathematical jewel. This flat, brass, disklike device was calibrated in degrees, which allowed travelers to measure the elevation of the sun or a star and calculate locations. Using this instrument, Muslim travelers could determine the exact direction of Mecca and the precise arrivals of sunrise and sunset, which were needed to determine the times for daily prayer. "For a long time the astrolabe was the pocket watch and the slide rule of the world," observes scholar Jacob Bronowski.[67]

Meanwhile, Muslim astronomers, using astrolabes and large quadrants and sextants, searched the night skies in an attempt to reconfirm earlier Greek findings of star and planetary locations. In the process, they also made new astronomical discoveries of their own. They studied sunspots, the length of the solar years, and the arrival of the longest and shortest days of every year. These stargazers also determined that the earth was a sphere. They calculated the length of one degree (1/360) of the earth's surface to be 56 ⅔ miles and reckoned the earth's circumference at about 20,000 miles. (The actual distance is about 26,000 miles.) This information helped Muslim mapmakers

An Arabian astrolabe from the eleventh century. This instrument was so valuable as a travel aid that Muslims called it the "mathematical jewel."

The Prince of Philosophers

In John L. Esposito's Islam: The Straight Path, *Avicenna, the great Muslim genius, recollects the studies he undertook as a teenager to prepare for a life of the mind.*

"I busied myself with the study of . . . commentaries on physics and mathematics, and the doors of knowledge opened before me. Then I took up medicine. . . . Medicine is not one of the difficult sciences, and in a very short time I undoubtedly excelled in it, so that physicians of merit studied under me. I also attended the sick, and the doors of medical treatments based on experience opened before me to an extent that can not be described. [Meanwhile] I carried on debates and controversies in jurisprudence [law]. At this point I was sixteen years old.

Then, for a year and a half, I devoted myself to study. I resumed the study of logic and all parts of philosophy. During this time I never slept the whole night through and did nothing but study all day long. Whenever I was puzzled by a problem . . . I would go to the mosque, pray, and beg the Creator of All to reveal to me that which was hidden from me and to make easy for me that which was difficult. Then at night I would return home, put a lamp in front of me, and set to work reading and writing . . . I went on like this until I was firmly grounded in all sciences and mastered them as far as was humanly possible. . . . Thus I mastered logic, physics, and mathematics."

The Muslim philosopher Avicenna mastered numerous disciplines and awed the public with his great intellect.

Arabian astronomers made substantial scientific discoveries as they studied the night skies using a plethora of instruments.

The greatest number reckoner of them all was al-Khwārizmī, the Father of Arithmetic, who lived in the mid–ninth century. This master mathematician drew up the earliest known trigonometry tables. His astronomical calculations were used by astronomers from Spain to Asia. Al-Khwārizmī also improved *aljabr*, a mathematical system better known in the West as algebra. His book, *Hisab al Jabr wa'l-Mugabala*, which means "the art of bringing together unknowns to match a known quantity," was translated into Latin during the twelfth century and introduced into Europe, where it remained a major textbook for the next four hundred years.

Al-Khwārizmī cultivated the use of the idea of zero among Muslim mathematicians. The circle-shaped symbol for zero in Arabic is *sifr*, which means "empty." The English word *cipher*, meaning "zero," is derived from its Arabic source.

establish standards for longitude and latitude lines.

Mathematics

Along with these scientific advances, Muslims made great strides in mathematics. To simplify and expedite calculations, Muslim mathematicians borrowed numerals from India and developed a system of number writing now known as Arabic numerals and still used around the world. Across the face of Islam, Muslims also perfected calculus, analytical geometry, and plane and spherical trigonometry.

Arabic Love of Words

Perhaps the most esteemed of all arts among Muslims is use of the Arabic language. To Muslims, after all, this was the language spoken by Muhammad to communicate the divine messages of Allah. Many Muslims insist that the Koran be read aloud because the beauty and majesty of both the written and the spoken word put believers into a spiritual mood that places them closer to God.

Early Arabs spoke many dialects, but common to many of them was a poetic language that pastoral tribes highly esteemed. Arabs not only considered poetry a thing of beauty, but they also deemed the ability to compose and speak poetry a manly virtue. Poets, like warriors, received high status in Arab lands. Men often gathered in tents during cool desert nights to challenge one another to poetry duels. Observes author Khairat Al-Saleh, "The Arabian poet was regarded as one gifted with knowledge beyond ordinary humans and as his function developed, he began to assume many roles, including that of leader, spokesman, soothsayer, teacher, chronicler and priest."[68]

Even as recently as the eve of the Persian Gulf War of 1991, poets appeared on both Iraqi and Saudi television networks and beamed poetic boasts and curses at each side in a time-honored tradition.

Perhaps the most popular and well-known collection of poems ever produced by a Muslim was the *Rubáiyát*, meaning "four-line verses." This work, composed by Persian mathematician Omar Khayyám, has delighted readers ever since its creation in the eleventh century.

Arabic Prose

Though poetry and the spoken word were time-honored forms of expression among Arabs, the elevation of written prose was relatively new. During the golden age Muslim writers penned adventure tales, proverbs, and moralistic stories with Islamic themes. The most famous nonreligious work is probably *A Thousand and One Nights*, which contains, among other tales, the beloved stories of Ali Baba, Aladdin, and Sinbad.

A special type of prose literature called the *adab* developed during the Abbasid period. Writers of this literary form delved into philosophical and moral issues, using Islam as their guide. One of the best writers in this tradition was al-Jāhiz, who penned these words:

A man who is noble does not pretend to be noble, any more than an eloquent man feigns eloquence. When a man exaggerates his qualities it is because of something lacking in himself; the bully gives himself airs because he is conscious of his weakness. Pride is ugly in all men . . . ; it is worse than cruelty, which is the worst of sins, and humility is better than clemency [mercy], which is the best of good deeds.[69]

The Muslims also excelled in the writing of history. One of Islam's greatest scholars, Ibn Khaldūn, used the rational philosophical approach refined by the Greeks to write his historical accounts. Somewhat of a social scientist, Ibn Khaldūn tried to discover underlying laws of nature that fashioned human events. Rather than merely record events, he sought to interpret human actions by taking into account a region's culture, geography, and socioeconomic characteristics. While this is a standard procedure today, it was something new in Ibn Khaldūn's time.

Decorative Arts

Some scholars believe that since so many ethnic and cultural groups make up the Muslim world, there is no single thing that can be specifically described as Islamic art. Nonetheless, others point out, there is a distinctive flavor that has developed through the centuries.

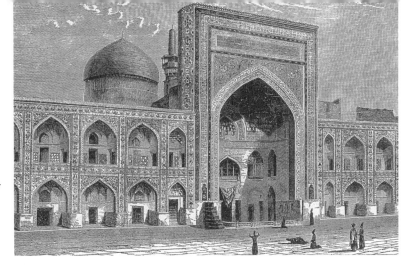

Muslim architects designed splendid buildings as places of Muslim worship. The interior (below) and exterior of a mosque show the characteristic dome and decorative tiles.

it adorned many paintings, ornaments, coins, and even walls of ornate buildings found in the Muslim world.

In many palaces found in the world of Islam, wall paintings depicting battles, animals, and people can be seen. But this is not the case in buildings that had a religious significance. Islam frowns on the glorification of the human body, as practiced by the early Greeks in their arts. Many students of Islamic law, or jurists, insisted that only God has the authority to create life. The act of creating humans in art, therefore, is seen as inappropriate for mortals. So Muslim artists emphasized the use of geometric designs and Arabic script in their places of worship.

Wherever Islam has spread, a distinctive architecture has gone with it, revealing a palette of influences absorbed from Egypt, Mesopotamia, Syria, Byzantium, and India. Characteristic of this blend are huge rounded domes and pointed towers, or minarets, mosaic tiles, arcades, walls covered with marble or colored glass, patios, and tiled roofs that adorn many mosques.

Arabic aesthetic sensibility is also evident in Muslim handcrafted items. Skilled

For instance, Arabic script itself has been transformed into a form of visual art. Used as both a decoration and calligraphy, artisans produced world-class rugs, tapestries, carpets, pottery, glassware, wood carvings, silk cloth, embossed linen, leather products, paper, metal goods, and even a fine grade of steel.

The Rule of Religious Law

One of Islam's greatest achievements was in the field of law. Like that of the Roman Empire, Islamic law was highly developed. Un-like much of the judicial system in Europe, however, Islamic law—Sharia—was rooted in religious concepts, as established in the Koran and the Hadith. In fact, two hundred of the six thousand verses of the Koran are laws. Unlike legal systems found in the West, the Islamic body of law concerns not only a person's relationship to neighbors and community, but also to Allah.

As Islam matured through the centuries, legal problems developed that proved increasingly hard to find precise Koranic answers to. Thus, Muslim legal scholars gradually developed the idea of

The Rise of Arabic Numerals

In his classic work The Ascent of Man, *scholar Jacob Bronowski offers this clear explanation of why Arabic numerals were superior to the older Roman style.*

"The most important single innovation that the eager, in-quisitive, and tolerant Arab scholar brought from afar was in writing numbers. The European notation for numbers then was still the clumsy Roman style, in which the number is put together from its parts by simple addition: for example, 1825 is written as MDCCCXXV, because it is the sum of M = 1000, D = 500, C + C + C = 100 + 100 + 100, XX = 10 + 10, and V = 5. Islam replaced that by the modern decimal notation that we still call 'Arabic'. . . . To write 1825 [in Arabic numerals], the four symbols would simply be written as they stand, in order, running straight on as a simple number; because it is the place in which each symbol stands that announces whether it stands for thousands, or hundreds, or tens, or units.

However, a system that describes magnitude [quantity] by place must provide for the possibility of empty places. The Arabic notation requires the invention of a zero. . . . The Arabs brought the decimal system from India about A.D. 750, but it did not take hold in Europe for another five hundred years after that."

analogies, a system of legal reasoning that used examples from the Koran similar to the case before the judges. This excerpt from the writings of twelfth-century legalist Burhan al-Dīn al-Marghinani illustrates such an analogy:

> Marriage with a woman of the Book [Jew or Christian] is lawful, but not marriage with a Zoroastrian woman, according to the statement of the Prophet, "Treat them as you would treat People of the Book, but do not marry their women or eat the animals they slaughter.
>
> Similarly marriage with an idolatress is forbidden, until she accepts Islam or a religion of the Book."[70]

Primarily, Islamic jurists recognized five different categories of human conduct. The first category dealt with acts that demanded absolute duty from Muslims. Those who did their duty were eligible for rewards; those who failed could receive punishment.

Next, there was the area of commendable, or praiseworthy, acts. Persons who carried these out could be rewarded; but those who failed to act would receive no punishment.

The third category focused on permissible acts, while the fourth dealt with shameful, but not punishable, acts. The last category concerned forbidden acts that demanded penalty.

All these legal approaches and many more helped to give a sense of order and unity throughout the Muslim realm. Although in time Islamic law did absorb some legal concepts and procedures used by Roman and Byzantine jurists, it remained rooted in Islam.

Disorder Returns

Ironically, while Islamic culture flowered into a golden age, an array of hostile political and religious forces within the Muslim Empire began to challenge and disrupt the unity wielded by the authoritative Abbasids. Revolts, disputes, and confrontations fragmented the vast Islamic world. Faced with all these formidable problems, the Abbasids could do nothing to keep the pieces of their empire together.

6 Islam's Medieval Empires

The Abbasid dynasty, which reigned from A.D. 747 to 1258, was the longest in Islam's history. For centuries it functioned smoothly and efficiently. But beneath the surface, mistakes were being made that eventually brought about the collapse of Abbasid rule. One reason for this decline was that caliphs began to squander their wealth and power. "Overindulgence in liquor, lechery, luxury, and sloth watered down the royal blood, and begot a succession of weaklings who fled from the tasks of government," writes Will Durant.[71]

Later Abbasid caliphs indeed failed to provide basic government services. They did little to protect merchants from bandits or to maintain the canals and irrigation systems that are vital to any country in the parched Middle East. Famine, epidemics, and high taxes drained the energy and patience of Muslims throughout the realm. The economy slowly deteriorated.

Divisive social problems also emerged. Upper-class women who once enjoyed a high status in Islamic society now saw Abbasids diminish their standing. Some women, for example, were relegated to harems, or rooms where they were secluded from public view and kept for the pleasures of the sultan.

Religious feuding, especially the never-ending quarrels between the Sunni major-ity and the Shiites, continued to be a problem. The Ismailis, one of the richest, most influential groups among the Shiites, initiated revolts throughout the western realm of the empire.

Meanwhile, other religious groups grew restless. One of them, the mystical branch of Islam called Sufism, begun in the eighth century, openly turned against traditional Islamic teaching and sought a more spiritual approach. The group's name is probably derived from Sufi mystics who lived as hermits and wore wool garments, the word *sūf* being Arabic for "wool."

Though Sufi philosophy changed over the years, the essential belief is that a Muslim should seek detachment from worldly things in order to have communion with God. Al-Hasan al-Basrī, a religious scholar who lived in the eighth century, provides this sample of early Sufi thought: "Beware of this world (*dunya*) with all wariness; for it is like to a snake, smooth to the touch, but its venom is deadly. . . . The more it pleases thee, the more do thou be wary of it."[72]

Many Sufi holy men often encouraged followers to seek a personal relationship with Allah by entering a heightened emotional state. Some followers attempted this by meditating and fasting. Other Sufis became Dervishes, from the Persian word for beggar, who wandered the countryside performing mystical rites and dances.

In addition to these religious disputes, another interpretation of Islam generated controversy from the highest office of all.

Political Decay

In Baghdad, Hārūn ar-Rashīd's son, al-Ma'mūn who lived from 813 to 833 sped up the deterioration of the empire when he decided to champion a new religious philosophy called Mu'tazilah. Influenced by the ancient Greek thinkers, proponents of Mu'tazilah believed that the reasoning power of the human mind was equal in importance to revelations from Allah. Moreover, they held that God allowed humans to exercise free will and held them accountable for their actions. Sections of the Koran, they argued, should be taken as figures of speech rather than as literal words of God.

Such ideas infuriated traditional ulema, who openly voiced their opposition even at the risk of being imprisoned for disagreeing. Their protest escalated when al-Ma'mūn's brother, al-Mu'tasim, followed him to the throne and continued to support the Mu'tazilite philosophy. Eventually al-Mu'tasim was forced to surround himself with trained Turkish slaves for protection. Inadvertently, his decision helped to bring down the Abbasid caliphate. By 861 the Turkish military officers who commanded the caliph's bodyguards realized they now had the power to control the caliphs. In effect, the caliphs had become slaves to their own protectors. When the true weakness of the caliph's power became widely known, revolts against the government took place across the face of Persia.

Revolts!

The first sign that Abbasid control was losing power came as early as 756, when the Spanish Umayyads broke away. Abbasids saw their political power and authority disintegrate even more between 788 and 945 as rebellious Muslims in Iran, Syria, Iraq, Egypt, Morocco, and Tunisia formed semi-independent regimes.

Among these breakaway movements in Egypt and Tunisia were those led by the followers of Muhammad's daughter, Fātimah. Although these Fatimads failed to completely overthrow the Abbasids, they were able to gain control over a stretch of land that ranged from Morocco to Syria.

By the eleventh century the old Muslim Empire was severely fragmented. Nonetheless, a strong measure of cultural and spiritual unity and basic forms of Islamic way of life still existed in the splintered Muslim lands. And although politically divided, Islam was still potent enough to threaten Europe in three important regions: Spain, Sicily, and the Levant, an expanse of territory bordering on the eastern Mediterranean. And it was here in the Levant that the stage was being set for a catastrophic clash between Islam and its old rival, Christendom—the Holy Roman Empire in western Europe.

Ever since the seventh century, Muslims had controlled Jerusalem and the surrounding lands that once had belonged to the Byzantine Christians. Pious Christians throughout Europe were infuriated that the land where Christ had taught and died was ruled by non-Christians. With mounting dismay and anger, European Christians learned of increasing numbers of fellow believers in Middle Eastern lands who converted to Islam and adopted Arabic ways of life.

"The Christian European response was, with few exceptions, hostile, intolerant, and belligerent," writes John L. Esposito. "Muhammad was vilified as an imposter and identified as the anti-Christ. Islam was dismissed as religion of the sword led by an infidel [unbeliever] driven by a lust for power and women."[73]

During the eleventh century a nomadic people, the Seljuk Turks, roared into the eastern realm of the Muslim Empire. After conquering Persia, the Turks captured Baghdad in 1055.

Quite suddenly Turks replaced Arabs as the rulers of what remained of the Muslim Empire. But they did not abolish the Abbasid caliphate. Instead, Seljuks allowed the caliphs to remain in office to give the appearance of being in charge. The real power, though, was in the hands of a sultan, a Turkish ruler who ruled from behind the scenes.

An illiterate and warlike people, the Seljuks found the Sunni form of Islam to their liking. They quickly adopted the concept of jihad to justify their own ambitions—namely, to raid and conquer their neighbors. One of their major targets was an area brimming with wealth and potential booty—the world of Byzantium. In 1071 Turkish Muslims inched closer to this goal when they routed Byzantine troops at the Battle of Manzikert and sent a shock wave through the Christian world.

Clearly the Seljuk Turks were a rising power. Within a decade they controlled most of Asia Minor, which comprised the eastern half of the Byzantine Empire. Now they seemed poised to accomplish what Muslim Arabs had always failed to do: take Byzantium's capital, Constantinople itself.

Mounting Tensions Between Christians and Muslims

The stage was set for a violent showdown between two major religious powers: Islam and Christianity. The first major act of violence came when Christians initiated a fight, the Reconquista, to reconquer Spain in 1061. This war raged for centuries and resulted in Christian forces' ultimately reclaiming the Iberian Peninsula.

War fever intensified in Europe when desperate Christian leaders in Constantinople begged fellow Christians everywhere to help them ward off the menacing Seljuks. In 1095 Pope Urban II, the head of the Roman Catholic Church and possibly the most powerful man in Europe, made a fiery speech in southern France. He urged Christians across the face of Europe to march in mass to aid their Christian brethren who were being attacked in the Muslim lands.

His appeal worked. Europeans flocked by the hundreds of thousands to amass the mighty armies being formed to slaughter Muslims. "Like wild fire a strange psychological wave, centering in France, spread through Europe engulfing high and low, old and young and in some cases emptying whole villages of their populations," observes historian Philip Hitti.[74]

Christian leaders publicly insisted that the purpose of these so-called holy wars—the Crusades—was to provide Christians

Ostensibly a religious conflict, the Crusades erupted in the eleventh century, beginning a string of battles between European invaders and Muslim troops.

free and safe access to their holy shrines in Jerusalem, a city considered sacred by three faiths: Christianity, Judaism, and Islam.

The war fires of the Crusades, however, were being fueled by individuals who harbored other motives as well. Several French princes, for instance, planned to use the Crusades as a means of acquiring new territories in Muslim lands. Many Italian bankers and merchants in the growing seaports of Genoa and Venice saw holy war as a way to open up new markets in the Middle East. Some crusaders merely craved adventure.

Political reasons also lurked behind the Crusades. Pope Urban surely relished Constantinople's plea for help. For the previous eighty-six years, religious and political differences had split the Christian world. As a consequence, both Rome and Constantinople emerged as competing Christian capitals.

With Constantinople now in serious trouble, the pope realized that Rome had a great opportunity. By lending a hand in a time of need, Rome could reassert its authority over its rival when the fighting was over.

The Crusades also gave the Catholic Church a way of unifying feudal Europe, which had fragmented since the fall of Rome centuries before. During the Dark

Ages Europeans had warred against each other and kept the continent in turmoil. Now they could unite to war against the infidels of Islam.

The Crusades

In 1099 the Christians attacked and captured Jerusalem to establish what is known as a crusader state. Crusaders did more than liberate Christians, though. They also committed atrocities. Mobs of frenzied crusaders hacked thousands of Jews and Muslims to pieces, burned them alive, and enslaved survivors.

More bloodshed followed. Almost a century later, in 1187, Muslims led by Saladin, one of Islam's greatest military leaders, took back Jerusalem. The fall of the Holy Land shocked Europeans. "Who will give water to my head and a fountain of tears to my eyes that I may weep day and night for the slaughter of my people," wailed a new pope, Gregory VIII, who forged the Third Crusade to recapture the Holy City.[75] This crusade failed.

One crusade after another was launched from Europe for another hundred years. Each time, Muslim forces arose to meet the invaders from Europe. These bloody struggles were not always merely religious conflicts. In fact, some historians labeled the Fourth Crusade the "businessmen's crusade" because Christian troops ignored Muslim warriors and instead attacked and looted Constantinople. Here, they set up their own government and lucrative trade arrangements with eager merchants in Italy.

At the onset of their crusades, many Christians fully expected to encounter

In 1187, the mighty warrior Saladin led Muslim troops to victory in a quest to reclaim Jerusalem.

barbarians. Instead, they were shocked to find Islamic culture vastly superior to their own. Europeans gleaned much from their journeys into Muslim lands and changed the face of Europe when they returned home.

Returning crusaders, writes Thomas J. Abercrombie, carried with them Muslim ideas, such as

[the use of] improved armor and fortifications, military use of carrier pigeons and heraldry, knightly tournaments and concepts of chivalry. The

The Beauty of Constantinople

As recorded in Ernle Bradford's The Sundered Cross, *on June 12, 1203, crusader Count de Villehardouin offered this impression as he gazed from an anchored ship at the skyline of Constantinople, a city coveted by both Muslim and Christian warriors.*

"All those who had never seen Constantinople before gazed with astonishment at the city. They had never imagined that anywhere in the world there could be a city like this. They took careful note of the high walls and imposing towers that encircled it. They gazed with wonder at its rich palaces and mighty churches, for it was difficult for them to believe that there were indeed so many of them. As they gazed at the length and breadth of that superb city there was not a man, however brave and daring, who did not feel a shudder down his spine. One could not blame them, for never before in the whole history of the world had any men embarked upon so gigantic an enterprise."

A fifteenth-century view of Constantinople shows the high walls and towers that encompassed the prized city.

pointed arch, developed in Persia, provided an architectural key to building lofty cathedrals. New foods appeared on Europe's tables: apricots, rice and *sukkar*—sugar.[76]

In time these innovations helped to bring an end to the feudal system and the Dark Ages that had dominated Europe for centuries.

There was one thing that Christians could not take back to Europe: news of a final and decisive victory. Despite their repeated attempts, Christian forces failed to dislodge Muslims from the Holy Land and regain control of Jerusalem. By the 1300s the crusading spirit in Europe evaporated.

But Islam was headed toward more war. Hordes of dangerous newcomers were sweeping in from the east.

Danger and Destruction from the Mongols

The new invaders were called Mongols. Also known as Tatars or Tartars, these horseback-mounted Asian nomads poured out of Mongolia and spread terror and death as they plundered one land after another. Under the reign of Genghis Khan, the Mongols destroyed entire civilizations and killed hundreds of thousands.

Next, they hacked their way into Muslim lands. In 1258 they attacked Baghdad and massacred thousands, including the last Abbasid caliph, al-Musta'sim, and many of his family. They left Baghdad in flames, the great irrigation projects of the Tigris and Euphrates Rivers in ruins, and Abbasid rule destroyed forever.

"The Mongol destruction of Baghdad ended an important phase in Islamic and world history," argues Desmond Stewart. "No longer would an Arabic-speaking caliph, claiming descent from the Prophet's tribe, preside with charismatic [magnetically appealing] authority over the world's most powerful state and complex culture."[77]

The Mongol disruption of Abbasid rule meant that for a brief while Egypt served as the stronghold of the Islamic world. Here the Mamluks, another Turk-

Ferocious Mongol invaders struck terror in the hearts of those occupying the lands they coveted. In 1258, Mongols stormed into Baghdad, obliterating Abbasid rule forever.

Mongol Onslaught

As quoted in Bertold Spuler's History of the Mongols, *thirteenth-century historian Ibn al-Athīr provides this description of the destruction of Islam at the hands of Mongols and other invaders:*

"For several years I put off reporting this event. I found it terrifying and felt revulsion at recounting it and therefore hesitated again and again. Who would find it easy to describe the ruin of Islam and the Muslims . . . ? O would that my mother had never borne me, that I had died before and that I were forgotten! . . . The report comprises the story of a . . . tremendous disaster such as had never happened before, and which struck all the world, though the Muslims above all . . . . These [the Mongols] . . . spared no one. They killed women, men and children, ripped open the bodies of the pregnant and slaughtered the unborn . . . .

Now, then, to report how the sparks [from these events] flew in all directions, and the evil spread everywhere. It moved across the lands like a cloud before the wind. . . .

In the countries that have not yet been overrun by them [the Mongols], everyone spends the night afraid that they may appear there, too. . . .

Thus Islam and the Muslims were struck at, at that time, by a disaster such as no people had experienced before. Part of this was due to those accursed Tatars [the Mongols]. They came from the East and committed actions that anybody upon hearing will consider horrifying. . . . Part of this disaster is also due to the intrusion into Syria of the cursed Franks [crusaders] from the West, their attack of Egypt, and their conquest of the coastal strip of Damietta. They might even have seized Egypt and Syria had it not been for God's grace and his help against them!

. . . May God grant victory to Islam and the Muslims, for he is the most powerful help and support of Islam. If God wishes to inflict harm on a people, there is no way of averting it, and no one but he can intercede."

ish dynasty, took charge and kept the Mongols from any further intrusion into Islamic territory.

The Ottomans Emerge

Following in the wake of the Mongol invasion came Turkish invaders from Asia Minor. Among them were the fierce Ottoman, or Osman, Turks from central Asia who arrived in the mid-1300s. These fighters derived their name from their leader Osman, the first of thirty-six Ottoman sultans destined to rule the Muslim Empire for nearly six hundred years.

The Ottomans fancied themselves as *ghazi*, or ferocious Islamic warriors—hard men who had no qualms about leading holy wars even against fellow Muslims. They wrested power from the Seljuks and took control of the Muslim world from the Persian Gulf to the Nile. Next they conquered the Mamluks in Egypt and then drove the Mongols from the Middle East.

The Ottomans took away more than political power from their predecessors. They also adopted both the Islamic faith and the Arab language. As the new rulers of the Muslim Empire, the Ottomans combined military prowess with an Islamic sense of mission to become a new and formidable expander of the faith. The most famous of the Ottoman sultans was Süleyman the Magnificent, who by the mid–sixteenth century had overseen the recovery of much of the old Muslim Empire and the conquest of new lands in southeastern Europe.

The expertise of the Ottomans was war. Their military pride and glory was glorified in the Janissary Corps, Christian youths

Süleyman the Magnificent is remembered not only for his campaigns to reclaim Muslim territory, but also for fueling expansion into southeastern Europe.

whom the Ottomans took from their parents and reared and trained to become ferocious fighters for the ruling sultans.

Waging jihad, Ottoman forces incorporated important cities under their rule such as Mecca, Medina, Cairo, Damascus, and Tunis. Next to fall were Greece, Malta, Cyprus, Tripoli, the Balkans, and much of eastern Europe. Eventually Arabia and Muslim territory in Iraq fell into the hands of Islam's new rulers. Soon there was one more area—that elusive and important plum, Constantinople.

The Long-Cherished Prize Falls to Islam

On April 22, 1453, over one hundred thousand Ottomans with a fleet of 125 ships under the leadership of Sultan Mehmed II attacked Constantinople. By the end of the next day, the 1,124-year-old Christian Byzantine Empire, which had long survived one Muslim attack after another, came to a sudden end.

The victorious Mehmed II now renamed himself the Conqueror. He also gave Constantinople a new name: Istanbul, from a Greek word meaning "into the city," and ordered the destruction of all vestiges of Christianity. He then commanded his men to remake the city into a new capital of Islam.

Flush with success, the Ottomans spread Islam across the Bosporus Strait and tried to penetrate Europe, but they were halted by Christian European troops at Vienna, Austria, in 1527. Thus, once again Muslims failed to penetrate the heartland of Europe.

Muslims Invade India

As the Ottomans spread their rule over former Byzantine territories, other Muslim invaders were changing the face of northwestern India. As early as 711 Arab Muslims had arrived in the southern Indus River valley. At that time, though, Indian troops kept them at bay.

But the people of India were not to remain so fortunate. During the eleventh century a new wave of warriors began riding through the mountain passes of the Himalayas and penetrated northwest India. This time the intruders were Turks from Central Asia who had converted to Islam. Their mission to India involved more than a desire to spread a religious belief; they came also to plunder, kill Hindus, and destroy sacred shrines and temples.

To Kill a Son

This quote from Philip Hitti's The Near East in History *reveals 'Abbās the Great's ruthlessness, as recorded by 'Abbās's own biographer, Iskandar Munshi, in 1616.*

"Should he ['Abbās] command a father to kill his son, the sentence would be carried out immediately, even as the decree of destiny; or should the father, moved by parental tenderness, make any delay, the command would be reversed; and should the son then temporize [hesitate], another would slay both. By such awful severity the execution of his commands attain the supreme degree of efficiency and none dared hesitate for an instant in the fulfilment of the sentence inevitable as fate."

Mahmūd of Ghazni, a Muslim who led seventeen raids into northern India, observed:

> The whole country of India is full of gold and jewels, and of the plants which grow there are those fit for making apparel, and aromatic plants and the sugar-cane, and the whole aspect of the country is pleasant and delightful. Now since the inhabitants are chiefly infidels and idolators [idol worshippers], by the order of God and his Prophet it is right for us to conquer them.[78]

Between the late twelfth and fourteenth centuries, the Turkish Muslims moved deep into northwest India and set up many independent kingdoms, or sultanates, from which they ruled the conquered Hindus of India.

Spreading Islam in India

All too often the sultans of these Muslim strongholds meted out unspeakable cruelty and violence against their captives. Many of these Muslim leaders, in fact, be-

In 1453, Constantinople falls into Muslim hands when the ferocious Ottomans attack the city.

The beautiful Taj Mahal in India, built as a tomb for Shāh Jahān's wife. Today, it continues to awe visitors from around the world.

lieved it was their duty to kill non-Muslim Indians.

In 1398, Mongol plunderers from eastern Asia, led by a Muslim chieftain named Tamerlane, plunged into northwest India, killing Muslims and Hindus alike. One year after having caused massive property damage and loss of life, he and his forces left India. Turkish rule was also badly shaken.

During the late 1500s a fresh invasion of Mongol warriors who appeared in India overthrew the Turks. These newcomers were also Muslim converts. One of them was Bābour, who established the rule of the Mughul (Persian for *Mongol*).

Under several Mughul rulers Islam spread farther into India. One of the greatest of them was Akbar, an emperor noted for enlightened rule, good government, and an attempt to reconcile the animosities between Hindus and Muslims. Unlike many of his predecessors, he promoted re-

ligious tolerance and unity among his subjects. Many Muslim religious leaders, however, opposed Akbar's attempts, which they thought weakened Islam.

Other Mughul rulers were not as open-minded as Akbar. Shāh Jahān, for example, repudiated Akbar's tolerance toward Hindus when he came to the throne and demanded that Islam alone be India's supreme religion. To accomplish this goal, he ordered the destruction of Hindu shrines and the persecution of Hindus and Christians.

The harsh legacy of Shāh Jahān, however, is associated with a great architectural wonder created during his reign from 1627 to 1658. Jahān's wife died at age thirty-nine, while attempting to give birth to her fourteenth child. Heartbroken, Shāh Jahān ordered a magnificent tomb, the Taj Mahal, to be built in her memory. Made of ivory white marble and graced by stunning Muslim-inspired minarets, this ar-

Ottomans' Victory at Belgrade

This excerpt from Süleyman the Magnificent's diary, taken from Readings in World History, *concerns the siege of his forces on the Hungarian-Serbian border fortresses at Belgrade and Sabac in 1521.*

"On July 7, came news of the capture of Sabac; a hundred heads of the soldiers of the garrison, who had been unable like the rest to escape by the river, were brought to the Sultan's camp. July 8 these heads are placed on pikes along his route. . . . Suleiman [Süleyman] visits the fort, and orders the construction of a bastion [fortification] with a moat; he also commands that a bridge be built over the Save [River], so that his army may cross to the northern bank. . . . July 18. Day of rest. The bridge is finished; but the Save is flooded. July 19. The water covers the bridge so it can no longer be used. Orders to cross by boats. Provisions sent overland to Belgrade. July 29. Suleiman sets forth for Belgrade along the Save. July 31. He arrives before the walls of Belgrade amid the cheers of his army."

chitectural wonder still attracts visitors from all over the world today.

Shāh Jahān fell from power when his own son, Aurangzeb, imprisoned him. A religious Muslim fanatic, Aurangzeb took over his father's throne and exceeded his father's religious zeal by spending twenty-six years and a vast amount of resources in a grand, bloody, and futile attempt to conquer all of India and set up an exclusively Muslim nation. Instead, he only ended up wasting many lives and bankrupting and weakening India.

A Clash of Religious Beliefs

For centuries Indian society had been able to assimilate waves of nomadic peoples and invaders. But Muslims proved to be very different. Their rigid Islamic beliefs put them at odds with the established cultural patterns of India. Perhaps no two other religions could contrast more than Hinduism and Islam did. For one thing, most Muslims looked down on India's Hindus and considered them lowly infidels, or nonbelievers. Hindus took a polytheistic approach to the understanding of God, whereas Muslims believed in one god. The Hindu representation of God in many ways—many of them in human form—also offended the Muslims.

Hindus also accepted the concept of reincarnation of human life; Muslims, on the other hand, insisted that every person had but one perishable life. Muslims also saw nothing wrong with eating meat, a practice that disgusted and offended many vegetarian Hindus. The Muslim aversion to alcohol was not shared by Hindus.

An ancient society, India was divided into four main castes, or classes, which in turn developed into over two thousand subcastes. This rigid social system ranked people by social, economic, and religious importance. At the bottom of the caste system was a class of people so despised that they were literally considered untouchables.

Muslims spurned the caste system; instead they stressed the Islamic values of equality and brotherhood to all who submitted to Allah. Eventually this promise of equality attracted poverty-stricken Hindus who felt hopelessly trapped in a lowly caste. Their conversion to a foreign religion, however, enraged other Indians.

Out of this collision of Islam and Hinduism came a new religion around 1500: Sikhism. This new faith "was an effort to find a ground beyond the conflict of Hindu and Muslim," points out University of Florida professor of religion Gene R. Thursby, "and one that was based on the viewpoint of some Indian sages that the divine reality is beyond all human efforts to picture or represent it."[79]

A Hindu holy man who founded Sikhism put it this way: "There is no Hindu," he said. "There is no [Muslim]. There is One God, the Supreme Truth."[80]

Nonetheless, the Sikhs remained a minority. The two great forces of Islam and Hinduism continued to divide the peoples of India.

The Safavids

No matter where Islam existed during these turbulent medieval times, the faith-

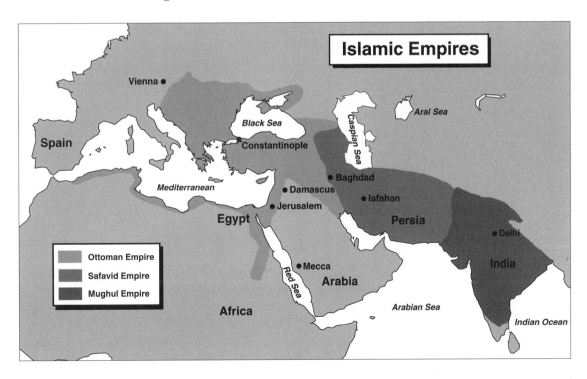

ful were usually split into at least two rival religious groups. In most Muslim lands the majority was the Sunni, who believed that rightful succession began with Abū Bakr and those caliphs who came afterward. The minority was almost always the Shia, those Muslims who believed that such authority belonged to descendants of 'Alī, Muhammad's son-in-law.

In Persia the story was different. Here, during the fifteenth century a powerful and determined religious minority outmaneuvered and overpowered the Sunni. For the previous two hundred years, followers of a puritanical form of Islam that was enriched with elements of Sufism eventually mingled with Persia's Shiites, who advocated a particularly fanatical and messianic, or crusading, version of Islam. As a result of this union, a new Islamic movement evolved in Persia with its own martyrs, customs, and celebrations.

In 1501, Ismā'īl Safavi, leader of the Safavid family, proclaimed himself shah of Iran and led adherents of this new Islamic religious force in a bold takeover of all Persia. His claim to authority was steeped in an old Shia belief. Many Shiites maintained that God had appointed a spiritual leader and interpreter of his revelation to Muhammad: a sinless leader, an imam who comes from the line of 'Alī. The twelfth descendant in this line, they say, disappeared in the ninth century. Members of a Shia movement called Twelvers, however, believe this imam still exists in a state of occultation—hidden from view— until he reappears in the future, when he will deliver the world from injustice and unrighteousness.

Ismā'īl Safavi claimed that as a descendant of the twelfth, hidden, imam, he was the rightful spiritual and political leader of Islam. He and other Safavid rulers who succeeded him called themselves the Shadow of God on Earth. Ismā'īl made Twelverism Shia the official religion of what became known as the Safavid movement. He suppressed all dissent and ordered all other forms of Islam destroyed. Writes historian William H. McNeill:

> Victory followed victory, until by 1506 the entire Iranian [Persian] plateau was united under the new conqueror. In 1508, Ismail asserted his power over Baghdad and most of Iraq, and in 1510 he administered a drastic defeat to the Uzbeks of *Transoxiana*, thereby securing his eastern frontier.[81]

Inspired by the Safavid Empire, Shia minorities in other Muslim lands launched revolts against their rulers. For decades frequent hostilities flared up between Safavid rebels and the Ottoman Empire. The psychological and spiritual scars from these conflicts ran deep. In fact, a rift between Sunni and Shia groups continues to be a major disruption in the world of Islam today.

Shah 'Abbās

The Safavid Empire reached its height under the leadership of Shah 'Abbās who ruled from 1586 to 1628. "'Great' became Abbas' title and great he was in energy, determination and even in ruthless jealousy," writes historian Philip Hitti. "He murdered one of his sons and blinded two others, as their popularity reached a point which did not suit his convenience."[82]

Cruel and ruthless, 'Abbās was also a forceful leader who successfully drove out

Turkish forces that occupied part of Persia. He oversaw massive building projects—schools, mosques, hospitals—and many needed economic and governmental reforms. Isfahan, his capital, was called a wonder of the world. Like the Ottomans, he incorporated the ulema into a state bureaucracy to weld together the political and religious sectors, which helped to make 'Abbās's reign one of greatness.

So dependent were Persians on 'Abbās that when he died, the Safavid Empire began to decline. No heir was capable of saving it.

"Abbas' immediate successor, his grandson Safi," writes Philip Hitti, ". . . distinguished himself by a wholesale execution of members of the royal family, male and female, together with most of the generals and counselors who had contributed to making his grandfather's reign the illustrious reign that it was."[83]

The Legacy of Islam's Power Centers

During the sixteenth century Islamic power reached a pinnacle through the harmony of Muslim power centers: the Ottoman Turkish Empire, the Persian Safavid Empire, and the Mughul Empire in India.

"Despite variations and the individual policies of some rulers, the imperial Ottoman, Safavid, and [Mughul] sultanates demonstrated a somewhat common Islamic ideological outlook and approach to state organization, support, and use of Islam," writes John L. Esposito.[84]

Islam's greatness would not last. A new challenge was on the way that would flatten the Muslim world. This time it was a revolution—not one of people and religions but, rather, one made by machines.

7 Imperial Islam in Decline

Despite centuries of bloody revolts, foreign invasions, and internal religious disputes, Islam remained an enduring and dynamic faith for millions of people. But during the seventeenth century its political, military, and economic clout began to wither.

One of the first signs of trouble came in 1699 when the Ottoman Empire lost a war with the Austrian Empire. The resulting peace treaty forced the defeated Turks to yield nearly all of Hungary to the Austrians. Many independence-minded Muslim leaders within the Ottoman Empire quickly took advantage of the apparent Ottoman military weakness and staged breakaway revolts against Turkish rule. Lawlessness soon plagued the empire.

Muslim rule in India was also in trouble. After Aurangzeb's death in 1707, the subcontinent sank into chaos and decline as Hindus, Muslims, Sikhs, and armed forces from Great Britain and France battled for control of India. Ultimately, Great Britain became India's master and ruled over the subcontinent until the late 1940s.

Meanwhile, the Persian Safavid Empire, which was still in decline following the death of 'Abbās, fell even further into disorder in 1709 when it was shaken by an Afghan revolt. For the next twenty years, Afghans, Russians, Turks, and others struggled to control various areas of the crumbling empire.

Fueling the disintegration of all three of these empires was a common and potent force: the growing economic power of western Europe.

Eclipsed by Christian Europe

For centuries the varied economies of the Muslim world had prospered from the output of quality handmade products, arts, crafts, and agricultural goods that were distributed and sold across Islam's far-reaching trade routes. But by the eighteenth century western Europeans were undergoing a major industrial revolution that enabled them to economically overshadow most countries of the world, including those ruled by Islam.

This transformation was made possible by a combination of rapid technological advancements such as steam engines and mechanized spinning and weaving machines, skilled labor, the rise of capitalism, and world exploration. All of these factors meant that European industries could produce vast amounts of machine-made products that were far cheaper than those produced by Muslim artisans. Across the

*The Industrial Revolution in Europe fueled the decline of the Muslim empires,
which could not keep pace with the onslaught of European products
bombarding the world market.*

Muslim world merchants and businesses began to fail as competitive European products appeared in the markets and shops of the globe.

"Throughout the eighteenth century, Moslem economies (save fringe areas of Africa and remote islands of southeast Asia), like Moslem politics, were everywhere shrinking and crumbling before the European onslaught," writes William McNeill.[85]

And by 1830, adds McNeill, the high quality of life that Muslims had enjoyed for centuries was in noticeable decline. This downfall coincided with the rise in power of a Christianized Europe. Industrialization had given Europeans something more than economic power, however.

Now, flush with wealth, confidence, and a desire for more material rewards, many European nations began to nurture imperial and colonial ambitions. Sturdy seagoing ships gave them not only access to international resources and markets, but also dominance of the world's sea lanes.

In contrast, Islam seemed to be stagnating, if not losing ground. It experienced no significant industrial breakthroughs. Because of its theocratic nature it did not allow, as Europe did, the accumulation of great amounts of capital needed for huge business enterprises. And unlike England, France, Holland, and Portugal, Islam did not dispatch ships to the New World to obtain natural resources, overseas markets, colonies, and strategic advantages. It experienced no Renaissance, no Age of Reason, no Enlightenment—all phases of development leading to the Industrial Revolution in Europe. Writes Robert Payne:

> Once more Islam was slowly dying. [It] . . . seemed to have lost its savor [delight]. There was no art, no religious feeling, only the interminable [endless] and empty recitation of the Quran. The great thinkers of the past were no longer read, their books gathering dust in the libraries. . . . The Ottoman Turks had failed to fertilize the Arab genius. The sun had gone down, and there seemed no hope of a dawn.[86]

Roused from Stupor

In 1798 something at last did happen to awaken Islam from its stupor when a French army under the command of Napoléon Bonaparte occupied Egypt, an independent Muslim territory. Napoléon's reason for being in Egypt is not clear. He may have hoped to interfere with British activities in the region. At any rate, the French intruders easily rebuffed Turkish troops that were sent to oust them. Not long afterwards though, Napoléon ran into strong resistance on land and defeat by the British at sea. With his supply line severed, he evacuated with the bulk of his troops and returned to France. Muslim forces easily routed the troops he left behind in Egypt.

Napoléon's brief presence had taken a toll. "The Napoleonic armed inroad into Arab territory was the first of its kind following the Crusading days," argues Philip Hitti. "It set a chain reaction—on both the political and intellectual levels—that has not yet ceased."[87]

When the French returned in 1830 and began to fight for control of Algeria, Muslim leaders everywhere realized that some sort of reform was needed to regenerate the Muslim world to stave off France and any other aggressive Western nations.

Islam's Conservative Response

Muslims everywhere were in shock. Why had the Christian world surpassed Islam? they wondered. How could this have happened to those who submitted to Islam? Was Islam itself destined for oblivion? Is-

Napoléon Bonaparte in Egypt. His brief occupation of Arab territory increased Muslims' concern over possible invasion by other aggressive Western nations.

An Assault on Delhi

In 1739 an Afghani robber named Nāder Shāh entered Delhi, where his men sacked the city and massacred fifty-thousand people. David Carroll's book, The Taj Mahal, *contains this eyewitness report:*

"On the morning of Sunday, 11 March 1739, an order went forth from the Persian Emperor for the slaughter of the inhabitants. The result may be imagined. One moment would seem to have sufficed for universal destruction. The Chandi Chowk, the fruit market, the Dariba Bazar, and the buildings around the Masjd-i-Jama were set afire and reduced to ashes. The inhabitants, one and all, were slaughtered. Here and there some opposition was offered, but in most places people were butchered unresistingly. The Persians laid violent hands on everything and everybody; cloth, jewels, and dishes of gold and silver were all acceptable spoil."

lamic intellectuals and leaders probed these vexing questions to find answers that they hoped would lead to salvation.

One group of religious leaders decided that Islam had lost its way since the early days of Muhammad's teachings. Over the centuries, they argued, Muslims had deviated from the Straight Path set down by Muhammad. Too much reverence was now being given to various holy men and saints rather than to the prophet Muhammad and Allah. Therefore, the solution to Islam's distress, argued some, was to rely on traditional religious and ideological, or cultural, modes of thinking, rather than independent thought. Believers, they argued, must return to the true teachings of Muhammad to reclaim Allah's blessing.

A leading advocate of this way of thinking was eighteenth-century Muhammad ibn 'Abd al-Wahhāb, a holy man in

central Arabia. A highly educated Muslim leader, al-Wahhāb was appalled at the backwardness and level of superstition that dominated so much of Arabia. His solution called for a clear and deliberate repetition of the past. If Muhammad had led a spiritual, social, and moral revolt against the Quraysh centuries before, then it was up to al-Wahhāb to lead a new one to cleanse a modern Arabia. Many of al-Wahhāb's ideas were based on the doctrines of a fourteenth-century thinker, Ibn Taymīyah, who wrote: "[T]hose who part with the Prophet and follow a way other than that of the faithful . . . have broken with him and exposed themselves to the divine threat."[88]

Thus, al-Wahhāb led a militant, zealous, and uncompromising movement to re-create a new *umma*, or community of believers. He also sought to purify Arabia of any ideas and even individuals that had strayed from the true path. This Wahhabi movement, as it was called, stimulated similar movements in India and Africa. It created the roots of a fundamentalist, or conservative, movement found throughout Islam today.

Although many Muslim scholars agree that conservatism is a common reaction to disorder throughout history, they also point out another possibility for a widespread Muslim conservative response. Islam had a long tradition of one caliph after another using force to take over the throne and then trying to justify his action by demanding that Muslims submit to a rigid, official form of orthodox thinking. Thus, in the eighteenth century, many Muslims were conditioned to respond to the European challenge as their ancestors had during past crises.

Other Approaches to Reform

Not all Muslim leaders agreed with the idea of trying to re-create history. They argued that Islam had to respond much more aggressively to the European challenge. Instead of turning to the past, they insisted, Muslims should take lessons from Europe. Then they could use this knowledge to strengthen and save Islam.

One of the first bold and forceful attempts at reform came in 1798 from a brilliant Turk named Muhammad 'Ali Pasha who had been dispatched to rebuff the French when Napoléon's forces landed in Egypt. When the French evacuated, he put together his own militia and successfully took over Egypt. For forty years he commanded Egypt as a semi-independent realm and introduced a series of modern-

izing reforms. He nationalized the production of indigo, grain, and sugar and implemented new farming methods. He imported factories, upgraded public education, built a naval fleet, began schools of medicine and engineering, created a new irrigation system, and fostered a public-works program.

Although many of Islam's political and military leaders outside of Egypt favored reforms emphasizing modernization—as Muhammad 'Ali Pasha had demonstrated—invariably the ulema and the Janissary Corps did not. Across Muslim lands these two groups blocked or resisted nearly every attempt at reform for nearly two hundred years.

"A blind conservatism, clinging to the crumbling landmarks of a vanishing social order, dominated the Moslem world until well past the middle of the nineteenth century," writes William H. McNeill.[89] In fact the Janissaries were so corrupt and entrenched in their ways that they assassinated Selim III, sultan of the Ottoman Empire, in 1808 when he sought to modernize the military.

Reform by Murder

Mahmud II, the nephew and admirer of Selim, decided to use treachery against those who would block reform when he became sultan. In 1826 he ordered newly recruited troops to open fire on the Janissary barracks. By the time the firing stopped, eight thousand Janissary soldiers lay dead. More were killed elsewhere in the empire. The ulema, shocked and intimidated by this bold and bloody action, said little in protest of Mahmud's actions.

Mahmud II promoted the modernization of his empire in a quest to ward off the encroaching European world.

Mahmud quickly set to work to modernize his empire. He brought in teachers from Europe and especially encouraged the teaching of French so that Muslims could understand the top literary, political, social, scientific, and technical journals of Europe. New technical schools appeared. Muslims also saw farming methods transformed and their military modernized. The urgency the government felt in promoting these reform efforts is evident in this excerpt from a royal decree issued in 1839, following Mahmud's death:

> All the world knows that since the days of the Ottoman state, the lofty principles of the Qur'an [Koran] and the rules of the *shari'a* were always perfectly preserved. . . . But in the last one hundred and fifty years, because of a succession of difficult and diverse causes . . . its former strength and prosperity have changed into weakness and poverty. . . . Full of confidence in the help of the Most High, and certain of the support of our Prophet, we deem it necessary and important from now on to introduce new legislation in order to achieve effective administration of the Ottoman government and provinces.[90]

Tanzimat

With the Janissary Corps gone, the less religious forces in the empire launched Tanzimat, or reorganization—a government attempt at copying European power structures. Abdul Mejid (1839-1861), a successor to Mahmud II, strengthened this movement by declaring the equality of all Ottoman citizens—non-Muslims included—and promised to protect the lives and property of all subjects. He set up military schools and a legal code rooted in the Code Napoléon created by the famous French dictator. School systems that were less religious in nature were established, and many government and military officials adopted Western clothing.

Increasingly throughout the nineteenth century, political reform gained acceptance in the corridors of power in Istanbul and among Turkish writers and thinkers, who were greatly influenced by European writers.

Nonetheless, as Muslim leaders turned to Europe for inspiration, conservative religious leaders continued to oppose nearly all reforms and tried to obstruct modern changes that they thought undermined the traditions of Islam.

The Sick Man of Europe

At the start of the nineteenth century, the Ottomans ruled over a vast empire that encompassed parts of Asia, Africa, and Europe. It was the last of the three great Muslim empires to still wield power and assert influence over much of the Islamic world.

But the Ottoman Empire was weak. It lacked unity. In addition, a series of inept sultans had lived in luxury and failed to tend to pressing economic problems or curb the corruption of government officials.

Although Muslims were the majority of subjects in the empire, Jews and Christians also existed, particularly in the Balkan Peninsula of southeastern Europe. Religious differences among these groups often boiled into violence and kept parts of the empire in turmoil.

In fact, the Ottoman Empire was also shaken by never ending ethnic strife. Despite the unifying aspects of Islam, Arabs, Syrians, Armenians, Egyptians, Greeks, and many other ethnic groups fiercely clung to their own languages, cultures, and grievances. Many, such as the Armenians and Greeks, despised Turkish rule and longed for independence. As the nineteenth century came to an end, they finally got their chance to try.

For decades, the emperors, or czars, of Russia had clashed with the Ottoman sultan over land and religion. By the mid–1800s Czar Nicholas IV felt confident enough of his empire's strength and the apparent Turkish weakness that he began referring to the Ottoman empire as "a dying man" or a "corpse." And this huge corpse, he insisted, should be carved up and controlled by the major European powers.

Russians claimed their real interest in the area resulted from a desire to protect Orthodox Christians who lived throughout the empire. Most other European leaders, however, balked at such an idea. British officials, for example, wanted the Ottoman Turks to remain in power. They knew the Russians really wanted control of Istanbul to take over the water routes connecting the Black Sea with the Mediterranean. That such a change was not in the interest of other European countries is evident in British diplomat Lord Palmerston's attempt to downplay the Russian cry of alarm: "All that we hear every day of the week about the decay of the Turkish Empire, and its being a dead body, or a sapless trunk, and so forth, is pure and unadulterated [complete] nonsense."[91]

Thus, in 1853 when Russia launched what became known as the Crimean War, Great Britain, France, and Sardinia rushed to aid the Turks. After three years of bloody fighting, this alliance checked Russia's advance and kept the shaky Ottoman Empire alive.

Although the Ottoman Empire survived, its dependency on Europe only underscored its weakness. Many Turkish leaders now hoped this flagrant lesson would convince Muslims everywhere that the ongoing reform process was vitally necessary to save the Ottoman-controlled Muslim world from extinction.

Al-Afghānī's Call for Reform

Among the many Muslim reformers clamoring for attention in the nineteenth century, one name stands out: Jamāl ad-Dīn al-Afghānī, a popular teacher, journalist, lecturer, political activist, and untiring wanderer throughout much of the Muslim Empire. Wherever al-Afghānī traveled, his message was the same: Muslims must set aside their differences and unite to ward off the European challenge. Islam, he said, was more than a religion; it was also a vast society. The best way to preserve Islam, he argued, was to adopt modern technologies and sciences that would aid, not hinder, the Muslim way of life. Had not Islam once flourished thanks to science and reason? Now was the time to embrace them again. He admonished both Muslim modernists and traditionalists to work together. Al-Afghānī argued:

> Unlike other religions, Islam is concerned not only with the life to come.

Islam is more: it is concerned with the believers' interest in the world here below and with allowing them to realize success in this life as well as peace in the next life. It seeks "good fortune in two worlds."[92]

Through his articles and pronouncements, al-Afghānī made a tremendous impact on the Muslim world. His disciples carried his work well into the twentieth century and helped to launch reform movements across the shattered Muslim Empire. One of these devotees was Muhammad 'Abduh, who believed that Muslims had to combine religious devotion with reform. He wanted to modernize an antiquated Muslim educational system and to purify the Arabic language, which he thought had lost its vitality and precision.

With the aid of Great Britain, France, and Sardinia, the Ottoman Empire survived the Crimean War.

In 1898 Qasim Amīn, an Egyptian judge and a follower of 'Abduh, caused a firestorm of protest with the publication of his book, *Tahir al-Mar'ah* (*Liberation of Women*). In this work Amīn argued that the traditional Muslim suppression of women was largely responsible for much of Islam's downfall. He contended that Muslim tradition shackled women and made them powerless. Their feelings of inferiority, he argued, hurt the family unit and damaged Muslim society. Amīn also opposed harems, polygamy, and the custom of making women wear veils and said that these practices violated the principles of the Koran.

"The distinctions made by men like Abduh and Amin, between what Islam had become and what it had once been and might be again, played an important part in the crisis of soul that troubled 20th Century Islam," observes Desmond Stewart.[93]

Despite such well-intentioned soul-searching, the Ottoman world faced an array of overwhelming political and military forces that threatened to destroy it once and for all.

More Muslim Losses

In 1877 Russia again picked another fight with the Ottomans, claiming that Turks were abusing Russia's ethnic cousins, the Christian Slavs in Bulgaria, who had revolted against Turkish rule. This time the Turks were defeated. The treaty that ended the war took control of Romania away from the Ottomans, as well as parts of Bosnia and Herzegovina, Cyprus, Montenegro, Bulgaria, and Egypt.

The Muslim world shriveled even more in the wake of the Balkan Wars of 1912 and 1913, when the Ottomans were forced to give up Albania and Macedonia. The only European areas that still remained under Ottoman control were Istanbul and a small nearby area.

Several European nations had already seized areas of the Muslim world in Africa. France, for example, occupied Algeria, Morocco, and Tunisia, while Egypt fell into the hands of Great Britain. Imperialistic Italy moved in on Tripoli, Libya. Persia was divided by Russia and Great Britain into so-called spheres of influence; each country avoided interfering in each other's realm of political and commercial interest.

The Ottomans had one last hope to stave off final collapse of their rule. In 1908 a group called the Young Turks, flush with patriotic zeal and Western ideas, took over the government and tried to modernize and revitalize Turkish military power. At the time, their efforts accomplished little.

Within this ever dissolving empire many ethnic groups, such as the Arabs, Armenians, Lebanese, and Syrians, spoke of revolt. They were encouraged by the success of the breakaway republics in the Balkan Wars of 1912 and 1913 and now threatened to bolt from the empire too. When the Turkish military cracked down on all budding revolts, it saved the empire, but only for the moment, for a new danger was fast arising from which the Ottomans would never recover.

Chapter

8 Islam in Modern Times

At the dawn of the twentieth century, the great industrialized empires of Europe raced headlong into the worst human-made calamity the world had yet known. Called the Great War, later World War I, this catastrophe also proved to be a major turning point for the Muslim world.

Ethnic, racial, and territorial disputes lay at the heart of the underlying problems that led to war. Powerful nations such as Great Britain, France, Germany, Russia, and Austria-Hungary had long rivaled each other for power and prominence. For decades these empires promoted extreme nationalism and created entangling military alliances while they competed ruthlessly against each other to obtain colonies, overseas markets, natural resources, strategic advantage, and political influence around the world. Many of their efforts focused on the Balkans and the remnants of the decaying Ottoman Empire.

The Ottoman Empire Crumbles

Meanwhile, internal dissent wracked Ottoman rule. Arabs within the Turkish provinces were weary and resentful of what they considered harsh and unfair treatment at the hands of the Turks. In 1913 an Arab congress met in Paris and demanded that the Ottoman leaders grant Arab peoples the right of self-government.

Turkish officials refused. Instead, they expected their Arab subjects to remain loyal and unify with them in a massive jihad against their European enemies when war finally broke out in 1914.

The Turks, however, failed to rouse their fellow Muslims. Instead, Arabs throughout the Middle East and North Africa supported the Allied opposition of Great Britain, France, and Russia against the Turks. Setting aside their longtime distrust of Europeans, Arab leaders hoped the Allies could defeat or at least weaken the Ottoman Empire enough to ensure Arab independence. British leaders exploited these hopes by encouraging various Arab groups to believe that if they successfully revolted from Ottoman rule, Great Britain would later recognize them as independent nations.

In 1916 the Arabs did initiate such a revolt, and when the Ottoman Empire collapsed two years later, jubilant Arab Muslims were certain that independence was near at hand.

They were wrong. Arabs soon discovered that the British had no intention of keeping their promises. Great Britain and France, in fact, had secretly conspired to split Arab lands once the war was over. A newly formed world body, the League of Nations, turned over the formerly owned Turkish lands called Palestine, Transjordan, and Iraq to Great Britain, while Syria and Lebanon went to France.

A stroke of the pen ended the Ottoman Empire forever. What remained of the Muslim world was a patchwork of provinces and hastily formed nations, most of which lay in the shadow of European power. Explains historian Albert Hourani in *A History of the Arab Peoples:*

> The whole of the Arabic-speaking world was now under European rule, except for parts of the Arabian peninsula. Foreign control brought administrative change and some advance in education, but also encouraged the growth of nationalism, mainly among the educated strata [levels] of society. In some countries, agreement was reached with the dominant power on the extension of self-rule within limits, but in others the relationship remained one of opposition.[94]

A Need for National Identity

During the postwar period, a spirit of nationalism emerged among the peoples of the Middle East. Creating nations, though, proved hard to do. Europe's imperial powers, for instance, had created arbitrary political borders for the new Muslim nations, which often meant that peoples of dissimilar backgrounds were grouped together within the same nation. Such was the case

in Syria, Iraq, Lebanon, and Jordan. The Kurds saw their homeland, Kurdistan, divided among Turkey, Iran, Iraq, and the Soviet Union.

Muslims faced another problem in their quest for nationhood and independence. A new form of European pressure had begun to haunt Muslim lands. What Western nations now craved was access to the vast oil fields being discovered in the Middle East. Using huge investments and other financial enticements, many European businesses and governments exerted great economic, political, and military influence over the small, weak, thinly populated, and newly formed oil-rich countries.

At first some Muslims welcomed the investments and new technologies that accompanied the influx of oil-hungry Europeans. Others, though, were angered by the Europeans' presence. Once again an old debate reappeared. Should Muslims ignore the West and cling to their past? Or compromise with the modern world? While conservative Muslim countries fretted over how to adjust to present realities, one country, observers say, nearly turned its back on Islam altogether.

The Rebirth of Turkey

Shortly after the end of the world war, a strong, aggressive military leader named Mustafa Kemal took power in Turkey. A veteran of the Young Turks revolt, Kemal concluded that the key to Turkey's salvation was to separate Islam from the systems of government and law. Turkey's laws, formerly based on the Koran, were rewritten to reflect basic concepts of the legal systems of Switzerland, Germany,

France, and Italy. Europe's Roman alphabet replaced Arabic script for writing Turkish.

In 1922 Kemal ended the sultanate; two years later he halted a 1,292-year tradition by abolishing the caliphate. Though Kemal was a dictator, he proclaimed civil rights for both men and women and arranged for the creation of a modern democratic constitution that provided for the elections of a president and lawmakers.

Kemal wanted more than just a split between church and state. He also tried to weaken traditional Muslim culture. Friday ceased to be Turkey's official prayer day. Women no longer were required to wear veils. Traditional Muslim clothes, in fact, were banned in public. In addition, Kemal abolished polygamy.

Kemal abolished something else: a militaristic empire. This move disappointed many Turks, who urged Turkey to rearm and reclaim lost territories. To them, Kemal made this clarification of policy in a 1923 speech:

> My friends, those who conquer by the sword are doomed to be overcome by those who conquer with the plough, and finally to give place to them. That is what happened to the Ottoman Empire. . . . The arm that wields the sword grows weary and in the end puts it back in the scabbard, where perhaps it is doomed to rust and moulder; but the arm that holds the plough grows daily stronger, and in growing stronger becomes yet more the master and owner of the soil.[95]

Although many conservatives condemned Kemal's high-handed reforms, other Turks admired them and proudly proclaimed him as Atatürk, Father of the Turks. Some of his more devoted admirers even formed a cult based on his personality to fill the leadership void created by the disappearance of the sultanate.

Atatürk's reforms never restored Turkey to the glorious heyday of the Ottoman Empire, but they did go far in modernizing and unifying his country. Turkey became a Muslim country far more westernized and much less Islamic than most of its Muslim neighbors.

New Muslim Nations

In 1922 Persia wrested control from its protector, Great Britain, and set out to create a new identity. Former army officer Reza Khan deposed the ruling Persian despot and installed himself as the country's absolute ruler, or shah. Like Atatürk, the shah wanted to modernize, industrialize, and westernize Persia, later called Iran, with a series of far-reaching legal, political, and social reforms. He, too, sought to reduce the power of the religious classes and weaken Islamic tradition. The shah encouraged his people to look to Persia's pre-Islamic past for inspiration for the future. Islamic conservatives were furious over this insult to their faith. Their anger would smoulder for a half century until it finally exploded in a violent backlash in 1979 against the modern state begun by Reza Khan, then known as Reza Shah Pahlavi.

Meanwhile, in Arabia a different sort of nationalism developed thanks to the actions of a ruthless and mighty tribal leader named Ibn Saʿūd. Observed American writer Ameen Rihani:

Tall of stature, muscular, sinewy, and of noble proportions . . . [Ibn Saʿūd] in anger, changes completely and suddenly. All the charm of his features gives way to a mordant savage expression. Even the light in his smile becomes a white flame.[96]

By 1934 Ibn Saʿūd was so powerful that he was able to use his own family name to redesignate the entire peninsula as Saudi Arabia. Inspired by the Wahhabi movement, Ibn Saʿūd imposed on his subjects a return to traditional Koranic principles. Saudi Arabian women, for example, unlike those in Turkey and Persia, now were forced to wear veils. Alcohol was banned. For many years record players and movie theaters were banned.

During the 1930s and 1940s nationalist movements resulted in independence from European control of varying degrees for the states of Egypt, Iraq, Yemen, Syria, and Lebanon. In Southeast Asia independence from Europe came to the largely Muslim populations of Malaya in 1957 and Indonesia in 1959.

Muslim-dominated Afghanistan also managed to greatly reduce British control, while in nearby India, Muslim leaders demanded something startling, bold, and potentially lethal that shook the world.

King of Saudi Arabia Ibn Saʿūd relentlessly pursued a return to traditional Islamic principles.

The Creation of Pakistan and Bangladesh

Soon after World War II ended, the British government decided to grant India its independence. "But British leaders hesitated to act, for they feared that once colonial rule ended, Hindus and Muslims would rise against one another," points out Gene Thursby. "During the declining years of British colonial rule, religious hatred and bloodshed had returned to mar the early steps toward democracy in India."[97]

Thus, to minimize the possibility of bloodshed, Great Britain agreed to a novel Muslim demand: the political and physical separation of the two religions. What India's Muslim leaders proposed was nothing less than the creation of a separate Muslim nation in northwest and northeast India as part of a larger plan to grant India independence from Great Britain. This Muslim dream became reality in

1947, when British authorities divided India into two dominions.

The biggest dominion—the huge land area today known as India—remained predominantly Hindu. The north, however, was divided into two parts, East Pakistan and West Pakistan, where Muslims were free to create the single Muslim state of Pakistan.

Under this agreement, Muslims could voluntarily uproot themselves from their jobs, homes, and neighborhoods throughout India and migrate to the newly created Muslim lands. Legions of Hindus and Sikhs, who lived in the areas designated for the creation of Pakistan, were allowed to move south.

What some called the greatest migration in history began in September 1947.

Over eleven and a half million Hindu, Muslim, and Sikh refugees flooded across the Indian subcontinent.

Flight Lieutenant Patwant Singh, who made reconnaissance flights over the massive relocation, recalls his impression upon looking down at the Punjab and seeing "whole antlike herds of human beings walking over open country spread out like cattle in the cattle drives of the westerns I'd seen, slipping in droves past the fires of the villages burning all around them."[98]

As feared, ancient passions and hatreds had flared during this human flood, and hundreds of thousands of Hindus, Sikhs, and Muslims murdered each other in a series of senseless riots, uprisings, and massacres. By the time the killing stopped, an estimated half million people lay dead.

With the creation of the independent Muslim state of Pakistan in 1947, hordes of religious refugees move from India into Pakistan and from Pakistan into India. Members of this mass exodus were the victims of violence and riots, and many perished.

Despite the trauma and bloodletting, Muslims achieved their goal: Pakistan became an independent Muslim state. But more problems soon materialized. Bickering broke out between East and West Pakistan. Adding to their problems was the fact that both lands were separated by a thousand miles of land belonging to India. Such a gulf prevented Muslims from ever developing a sense of unity and common interest. After years of political strife, East Pakistan violently broke away from West Pakistan in 1971 and formed a new Muslim country now called Bangladesh.

Disunity and strife had been common throughout much of the Muslim world during the period between the world wars. Apart from their successes in various nationalistic and independence movements, many Arabs and other Muslims argued and fought among themselves. On the surface it appeared that Islam, the once powerful unifying force, had shattered into a kaleidoscope of ethnic fragments ranging from North Africa to India.

Nonetheless, the idea of Muslim brotherhood's transcending political borders was not totally dead. In fact, throughout the nineteenth century a negative form of unity developed that bonded Muslims everywhere: a shared hatred and fear against an increasingly powerful enemy, the Jewish state of Israel.

The Rise of Israel

The origin of the ongoing bloody conflict between Israel and the Muslim nations dates back to A.D. 70, when Roman soldiers destroyed the original Jewish state in Palestine. As a result, many Jews fled for their lives and resettled in Christian Europe. Here, for centuries, the Jews struggled against waves of persecution, hatred, and systematic killings meted out by one European ruler after another.

By the second half of the nineteenth century, though, a new and militant mood

The Return of an Islamic Golden Age?

Albert Hourani's History of the Arab Peoples *contains an excerpt from* Signposts on the Path *by Egyptian writer Sayiid Qutb, who made this prediction.*

"The leadership of western man in the human world is coming to an end, not because western civilization is materially bankrupt or has lost its economic or military strength, but because the western order has played its part, and no longer possesses that stock of 'values' which gave it its predominance. . . . The scientific revolution has finished its role, as have 'nationalism' and the territorially limited communities which grew up in its age. . . . The turn of Islam has come."

In 1971 East Pakistani citizens rally in the streets, demanding independence from West Pakistan. East Pakistan declared its independence and became Bangladesh the same year.

had emerged among Jewish communities in Europe. Many Jews now supported Zionism, a growing social and political movement calling on Jews to leave Europe and resettle in their ancient homeland which they now called Zion (promised land).

In 1918 Zionist leaders skillfully persuaded the British to allow them to create a modern state for Jews in Palestine, which at the time was a British protectorate. The British, however, also assured Arabs living in the region that this Jewish settlement would not deprive them of their way of life.

The British promise was impossible to keep when Jewish immigrants appeared in the 1920s. From the start Arabs and Jews argued and violently struggled over land, religion, culture, and sovereignty. Resentment and conflicts only worsened when a new flood of Jewish immigrants poured into Palestine to avoid Hitler's death camps in Europe.

Neither Great Britain nor the newly formed United Nations came up with a satisfactory peace plan that could appease both sides. Meanwhile, Zionists called for unrestricted immigration to Palestine at

On the Road to Misery

In their book Freedom at Midnight, *authors Larry Collins and Dominique Lapierre offer this description of the misery encountered by India's religious refugees in 1947.*

"By day, pale clouds of dust [were] churned by the hoofs of thousands of buffaloes and bullocks. . . . At night, collapsing by the side of the road, the refugees built thousands of little fires to cook their few scraps of food. From a distance, the light of their fires diffused by the dust . . . merged into one dull red glow. . . .

Eyes and throats raw with dust, feet bruised by stones or the searing asphalt, tortured by hunger and thirst, enrobed in a stench of urine, sweat and defecation, the refugees plodded dumbly forward. They flowed on in filthy dhotis [loincloths], saris, baggy trousers, frayed sandals, sometimes only one shoe, often none at all. Elderly women clung to their sons, pregnant women to their husbands. Men carried invalid wives and mothers on their shoulders, women their infants. They had to endure their burden not for a mile or two, but for a hundred, two hundred miles, for days on end, with nothing to nourish their strength but a chappati [flat bread] and a few sips of water a day."

Refugees in the 1947 migration to and from India endured great hardship and suffering. This photo of Hindu women and children was taken after they arrived in India. Their husbands and fathers were all killed in the political strife that prompted their migration to Hindu land.

Soldiers of the Arab Liberation Army shell Jewish positions during the war that resulted when Jewish settlers created the state of Israel in 1948.

the end of the world war, which provoked Palestinian Arabs even more.

When Jewish settlers proclaimed the creation of the state of Israel in 1948, Arabs everywhere were especially incensed. They felt displaced and threatened by the never ending tide of non-Arab newcomers and the growing importance of the Jewish religion. Moreover, many also suspected that European powers had connived to set up the state of Israel to stealthily exert control over events in the Middle East. Once again Muslims feared that the West was outmaneuvering the forces of Islam.

An Arab Response

In 1948 a coalition of Muslim nations—Syria, Egypt, Transjordan, later called Jordan, Iraq, Lebanon, Saudi Arabia, and Yemen—formed the Arab League to oppose Israel.

The next year war broke out when seven Arab nations attacked Israel, the new name for Jewish Palestine. Arabs were shocked by the outcome of battle: Israel not only repulsed its enemies but also occupied half of the Arab portion of Palestine.

The war, however, actually settled almost nothing. Arab leaders refused to sign a peace treaty that required them to recognize the right of Israel to exist. Meanwhile, during the war hundreds of thousands of Arabs fled their homes to resettle in makeshift refugee camps in nearby Arab territories. Here, Palestinian hatred and frustration would fester and turn violent for decades to come.

Unquestioning sympathy for the Palestinian refugees and opposition to Israel united Muslims in North Africa, the Middle East, and elsewhere during periods of armed conflicts, retaliations, terrorist attacks, and full-blown wars in 1956, 1967, and 1973.

The Pan-Arab Movement

Following the end of World War II, many Muslim leaders throughout the Arabic-speaking world advocated a new type of nationalism. It relied on the assumption that all Arab people—no matter in which nation they happen to live—were unified by language, religion, and culture and should be part of one borderless Arabic nation, regardless of where they lived.

Such a concept had great appeal throughout the Middle East. In fact, writes Albert Hourani:

> The dominant idea of the 1950s and 1960s was that of Arab nationalism, aspiring towards a close union of Arab countries, independence from the super-powers, and social reforms in the direction of greater equality; this idea was embodied for a time in the personality of Jamal 'Abd al-Nasir [Gamal Abdel Nasser] ruler of Egypt.[99]

Nasser, in fact, transformed Egypt into a dictatorship and dreamed of creating one vast Arab nation that would range from the Atlantic Ocean to the Persian Gulf. For a while, his ideas also attracted many Muslims outside Egypt, who favored an Islamic and Arabic movement. Egypt became a new intellectual center at the mainstream of Arab life.

But the Egyptian pan-Arab movement did not last long. "The defeat of Egypt and

Gamal Nasser, Arab leader and Egyptian president. Nasser's vision of one united Arab nation appealed to many Middle Easterners in the 1950s and 1960s.

Syria and Jordan in the war of 1967 with Israel, however, halted the advance of this idea, and opened a period of disunity and increasing dependence on one or the other of the superpowers, with the USA in the ascendant," Hourani points out.[100]

This Six-Day War, as it was called, was yet another conflict in a seemingly never ending Arab-Israeli dispute. As a result of this conflict, Israel took control of Old Jerusalem, one of three cities considered holy by Muslims.

This move angered the entire Muslim world. No longer was the Arab-Israeli conflict limited to just Palestinian Arabs. Israel's action was interpreted as an affront to Islam. Now Muslims everywhere, from sub-Saharan Africa to south Asia to Southeast Asia and throughout the Middle East, united in their opposition to Israel.

Islamic scholar Bernard Lewis points out that this united response ignited a period of soul-searching and questioning among Arab leaders over how to respond to the Israeli challenge.

The Arab failures in the struggle against Israel, particularly in 1948 and in 1967, revived the great debate on what is wrong with Arab and, more broadly, Islamic society, and what can be done to put it right. Like the Turks after their failure to capture Vienna, so the Arabs after their failure to capture Jerusalem began by seeing this as a primarily military problem for which there was a military solution: bigger and better armies with bigger and better weapons. And when these bigger and better armies also failed, there was a growing willingness to listen to those who sought deeper causes and offered more-radical solutions.[101]

Attempts at those radical solutions would soon begin to materialize as the Muslim Middle East experienced something it had lost centuries before: prosperity.

Islam's Modern Revival

During the postwar years the world community took an increased interest in the religious conflicts of the Middle East be-

Israeli troops on march during the Six-Day War in 1967. Israeli forces emerged victorious, and tensions continued to smolder during the postwar years.

cause these clashes were intertwined with the production of a vital resource—petroleum. Thanks to major investments and technological expertise from European and American companies, vast oil reserves were being discovered, tapped, and exploited, especially in countries around the Persian Gulf. The world was willing to pay handsomely for this source.

The resulting surge of oil revenues meant a burst of prosperity, power, and strategic world importance for the Gulf states such as Iran, Iraq, Kuwait, Saudi Arabia, and the United Arab Emirates. By the mid–1970s, in fact, several nations of the Persian Gulf had the highest per capita income in the world.

This newfound wealth meant greater opportunities for Muslims to travel and study abroad or buy the products of new technologies such as radios, televisions, and cassette recorders and learn more about the outside world.

Did this sudden fount of wealth collide with the goals of Islam? Not necessarily, explains British journalist Peter Mansfield:

> There is nothing in the Islamic religion that opposes economic progress. On the contrary, the Holy Koran enjoins creative economic activity and hard work on every Muslim. At the same time, he must avoid . . . [showing off his wealth] and pay his taxes for the benefit of the poor. Wealth should be equitably distributed.[102]

Apart from this ideal, however, many Muslims saw their traditional beliefs and values greatly threatened by the temptations of wealth. Money now enabled affluent Muslims to sample freedom and materialism that the industrialized nations of Europe and North America had to offer.

Many Muslims felt exhilarated and liberated by this exposure to the culture of the West. On the other hand, Islamic conservatives were outraged and horrified. In their eyes Islam was once again under assault from anti-Islamic forces. Bad enough, they argued, that the great Muslim empires of the past were gone, but now Muslims were being deceived and exploited by Europeans and Americans. Worse yet, these same foreigners supported the hated Israeli Jews, who repeatedly humiliated Muslim warriors in battle.

Moreover, they argued, the new wealth was not being divided evenly, as Muhammad had once implored. In fact, the gulf between the rich and the poor in many Muslim lands constantly widened.

For all these reasons, traditionalists believed that by adopting the ways of the West, wayward Muslims were making a mockery of the one true faith—Islam. And this was blasphemy that could not be tolerated.

Throughout the history of Islam a backlash of furious conservatism arose when Muslim society seemed to leave the Straight Path. In the 1960s another such movement emerged as a major force in the Middle East. Called Islamic fundamentalism, it began with the fall of the Ottoman Empire throughout the shattered Islamic world. When it finally crystallized, it would shake the modern world.

The Rise of Militant Islamic Fundamentalism

During the late twentieth century a militant brand of Islamic fundamentalism rose to world prominence. Like other conserv-

During the Islamic revolution of Ayatollah Khomeini, pro-Khomeini forces prepare a bunker in front of Iran's parliament building.

ative movements throughout Islam's turbulent history, this one demanded strict adherence to the core beliefs and laws of Islam. Modern fundamentalists abhorred the separation of church and state that took place in Turkey and Iran. Islam, they insisted, is God's law and cannot be divorced from the affairs of state. They believed the ways of the Western world had corroded Islamic values and should be resisted at all costs. Many fundamentalists even denounced secular, or nonreligious, governments in Muslim lands and the industrial nations that supported them.

The response of the modern fundamentalist, says Islamic scholar Bernard Lewis, "is the old Muslim obligation of jihad; to wage holy war first at home, against . . . [false Muslims who ran the country] and then, having ousted them and re-Islamized society, to resume the greater role of Islam in the world."[103]

Fundamentalists had their best chance to put their ideas into action when Iran exploded in civil war in the late 1970s.

Revolution in Iran

Trouble had been brewing for decades in Iran. A growing number of Iranians agreed with Islamic fundamentalists, who bitterly opposed the pro-Western and modernization attempts made by the shah, Mohammad Reza Pahlavi, who continued the policies begun by his father in the 1920s. Conservative Muslims, many of them poor, interpreted the gleaming skyscrapers, foreign banks made possible by oil revenues, and the Western lifestyles of the very affluent as signs of decadence and evil. They especially hated the Savak, the shah's secret police, who used brutal repression against critics of the government, and the shah's backer, the U.S. government.

In January 1979 revolution shook Iran. Led by Ayatollah Khomeini, an aging Muslim holy man who had returned from exile, fundamentalists unseated the shah and imposed a militant theocracy upon the Iranian people. Radical Islam became a reality for the United States when Islamic revolutionaries held fifty-two American hostages for 444 days and began exporting fundamentalist revolution around the world.

Iran's Ayatollah Khomeini's call to arms helped ignite a war between Sunni Iraq and Shiite Iran. When the war ended in 1988, over a half million Muslims lay dead.

Khomeini expected a fundamentalist tide to sweep across Muslim lands in North Africa and the Middle East. To expedite this, sympathetic radical extremists waged their own brand of jihad in the form of terrorist acts such as kidnapping, random murder, bombings, and hijacking of commercial jets. Their prime targets were Israelis, Europeans, Americans, and any others who were viewed as enemies of Islam.

The Gulf War

In 1990 the Middle East exploded into what many Islamic experts feared would become a modern version of the Crusades. The conflict began when Iraq, under the command of dictator Saddam Hussein, invaded its oil-rich neighbor, Kuwait. One of Hussein's goals was to forge once and for all a farflung Arab nation and reestablish an Islamic empire.

His plans were thwarted, however, by an array of outside forces. To prevent Iraq from controlling the vital Persian Gulf and interrupting the shipment of oil, an international military force made up of twenty-eight nations, under the auspices of the United Nations and led by the United States, attacked Iraq.

At the onset of the Gulf War, many Middle East observers expected that de-

In Iran, chador-clad women take part in a rally to mark the fourteenth anniversary of the Islamic revolution.

In Kuwait, U.S. forces watch for snipers during the Gulf War, in which Saddam Hussein sought to re-create a powerful Islamic empire.

spite their differences, Muslims everywhere would rally together in a massive jihad to assist Iraq.

This prediction proved false. Muslims everywhere were greatly divided in their opinions concerning the war. Nonetheless, even those Muslims who opposed Iraq still felt the tang of defeat and humiliation inflicted on them by the superiority of non-Muslim forces. Suggests William Pfaff, a writer for the *New Yorker:*

> The result for Islam, over the last three centuries, has been repeated political and military defeats, which have produced cultural anxiety and frustration and have involved a form of intellectual and moral subjection to the West. However, the fundamentalist movements in Iran, Lebanon, and elsewhere refuse defeat.[104]

Experts expect radical Islam activity to continue for years. By 1995, for example, the governments of Egypt and Algeria were engaged in violent conflicts with militant Muslim groups that were determined to take over the government. Terrorist acts continued in many lands.

Most Muslims, of course, are not radicals or terrorists and deplore the use of violence against innocents. In addition, many Muslim scholars point out that terrorist acts, such as kidnapping, are inconsistent with Islam. According to Hadith tradition, writes Karen Armstrong, Muhammad has this to say about how Muslims should treat captives: "You must feed them as you feed yourselves, and clothe them as you clothe yourselves, and if you should set them on a hard task, you must help them in it yourselves."[105]

Islam's Growing Impact

Despite the disruptions of radical funda-mentalists, Islam remains a major religious force and ideology today. Compromising about 17.1 percent of the world's popula-tion, it is now the second largest religion on earth. Islam is also the world's fastest growing religion.

Immigration patterns have also made this the fastest growing religion in the United States, where it is joined by a uniquely American offshoot Islamic move-ment begun by Wallace Fard in 1930 called the Nation of Islam. Initially a so-cial-protest movement against what many

In New York, hundreds of Muslims gather to pray. Islam continues to be a major religion in the modern world.

Islam in America

In this passage from an interview in Steven Barboza's American Jihad: Islam After Malcolm X, *Louis Farrakhan, leader of the Nation of Islam in Chicago, offers this explanation of Islam's role in America.*

"Since the time of Prophet Muhammad, we have in America a new reality that came up. . . . We don't have any record of a prophet of Allah coming to the Native Americans. The Caucasians from Europe came here. They had the prophets but the scriptures of the prophets had long been corrupted. So what you have in America are Caucasian people who set up a nation and a government on the basis of a corrupted version of the Torah of Moses and the . . . [Bible] of Jesus. So here now you have a new nation that has no real contact with the true message of Moses, the true message of Jesus, even the true message of Muhammad. So now, who will bring the message to the West and establish it among the Native Americans, among the Chicanos, among the blacks, and among the whites? That person can never do that without divine backing, and we believe that as God in the past always raised His servants up from among the ranks of the oppressed—we believe that God has raised Elijah Muhammad up from among us, not as a prophet, but to bring us the message of Islam according to the condition in which he found us."

black Americans saw as a white-dominated society, its followers today are expected to identify with an ancient lost tribe of Muslims, as well as accept a blend of traditional Islamic social practices and a program of black separatism, self-defense, and self-discipline.

Whether Muslims follow the teachings of the Sunni, Shia, Sufi, Nation of Islam, or any other group found within the rich and varied tapestry of the Muslim world, they seek in Islam the same values cherished by the believers in the past. This major faith offers spiritual guidance, a strong ethical code, a guide for living, a rich heritage, a purpose for living, hope in the hereafter, and a spiritual fulfillment that so many people yearn for today in a troubled world.

Islam once spawned empires from North Africa to the Middle East, across eastern Europe and into India. Though its political and military power have waned over the centuries, its spiritual force commands respect from nearly a fifth of humanity. Such a powerful legacy grew from the revelations received by a single man in an ancient world.

Notes

Introduction: Allahu Akbar!

1. William H. McNeill, *The Rise of the West*. Chicago: University of Chicago Press, 1963, p. 421.

Chapter 1: The Origins of Islam

2. Huston Smith, *The Religions of Man*. New York: Harper and Row, 1958, p. 195.
3. Will Durant, *The Age of Faith*. New York: Simon and Schuster, 1950, p. 161.
4. Robert Payne, *The History of Islam*. New York: Dorset Press, 1990, p. 68.
5. Karen Armstrong, *Muhammad: A Biography of the Prophet*. San Francisco: Harper San Francisco, 1992, pp. 45–46.
6. Quoted in Armstrong, *Muhammad*, p. 73.
7. Quoted in Gilbert M. Grosvenor, ed., *Great Religions of the World*. Washington, DC: National Geographic Society, 1971, p. 226.
8. Desmond Stewart and the editors of Time-Life Books, *Early Islam*. New York: Time-Life Books, 1967, p. 14.
9. Quoted in Payne, *The History of Islam*, pp. 15–16.
10. Edward J. Jurji, "Mohammed Is His Prophet," in Grosvenor, *Great Religions*, p. 229.
11. Joel Carmichael, *The Shaping of the Arabs*. New York: Macmillan, 1967, pp. 24–25.
12. Quoted in Payne, *The History of Islam*, p. 25.
13. H. G. Wells, *The Outline of History*. Garden City, N.Y.: Garden City Publishing, 1920, p. 573.

Chapter 2: The Fundamentals of a New Faith

14. Stewart, *Early Islam*, p. 17.
15. Armstrong, *Muhammad*, p. 166.
16. Muhammad Zafrulla Khan, trans. *The Quran*. New York: Olive Branch Press, 1991, p. 259.
17. Armstrong, *Muhammad*, p. 230.
18. Quoted in Payne, *The History of Islam*, p. 68.
19. Khan, *The Quran*, p. 635.
20. Durant, *The Age of Faith*, p. 178.
21. John L. Esposito, *Islam: The Straight Path*. New York: Oxford University Press, 1991, p. 21.
22. Khan, *The Quran*, p. 8.
23. Khan, *The Quran*, p. 509.
24. Khan, *The Quran*, p. 349.
25. Khan, *The Quran*, p. 600.
26. Khan, *The Quran*, p. 216.
27. Quoted in John Alden Williams, ed., *The Word of Islam*. Austin: University of Texas Press, 1994, p. 50.
28. Smith, *The Religions of Man*, pp. 217–218.
29. Durant, *The Age of Faith*, p. 181.

Chapter 3: The Conquests of Islam

30. Quoted in Payne, *The History of Islam*. p. 35.
31. Quoted in Time-Life Books, eds., *Time Frame AD 600–800: The March of Islam*. Alexandria, VA: Time-Life Books, 1988, p. 37.
32. Armstrong, *Muhammad*, p. 162.
33. Quoted in Payne, *The History of Islam*, p. 47.
34. Carmichael, *The Shaping of the Arabs*, p. 34.
35. Carmichael, *The Shaping of the Arabs*, p. 35.
36. McNeill, *The Rise of the West*, p. 36.
37. Quoted in Payne, *The History of Islam*, p. 63.

38. Quoted in Armstrong, *Muhammad*, p. 256.

39. Quoted in Armstrong, *Muhammad*, p. 256.

40. Quoted in Armstrong, *Muhammad*, p. 257.

41. Quoted in Armstrong, *Muhammad*, p. 257.

42. Wells, *The Outline of History*, p. 582.

43. Quoted in George Seldes, *The Great Thoughts*. New York: Ballantine, 1985, p. 314.

44. McNeill, *The Rise of the West*, p. 426.

45. Carmichael, *The Shaping of the Arabs*, p. 65.

46. Khan, *The Quran*, p. 30.

47. Khan, *The Quran*, p. 38.

48. Dilip Hiro, *Holy Wars: The Rise of Islamic Fundamentalism*. New York: Routledge, Chapman, and Hall, 1989, p. 13.

49. Quoted in Payne, *The History of Islam*, p. 105.

Chapter 4: The Splintering of Islam

50. Quoted in *Time Frame AD 600–800*, p. 41.

51. Quoted in Peter Mansfield, *The New Arabians*. Chicago: Ferguson Publishing, 1981, p. 26.

52. Quoted in Payne, *The History of Islam*, p. 104.

53. Quoted in Payne, *The History of Islam*, p. 109.

54. Quoted in Payne, *The History of Islam*, p. 111.

55. Quoted in Payne, *The History of Islam*, p. 115.

56. Stewart, *Early Islam*, p. 61.

57. Payne, *The History of Islam*, p. 118.

58. Quoted in Durant, *The Age of Faith*, p. 193.

59. Quoted in Payne, *The History of Islam*, p. 133.

60. Durant, *The Age of Faith*, p. 194

61. Durant, *The Age of Faith*, p. 196.

62. Stewart, *Early Islam*, p. 53.

Chapter 5: The Abbasid Golden Age

63. Philip K. Hitti, *The Near East in History*. Princeton, NJ: Van Nostrand, 1961, p. 243.

64. Quoted in Durant, *The Age of Faith*, p. 243.

65. Quoted in Seldes, *The Great Thoughts*, p. 26.

66. Durant, *The Age of Faith*, p. 245.

67. Jacob Bronowski, *The Ascent of Man*. Boston: Little, Brown, 1973, p. 166.

68. Khairat Al-Saleh, *Fabled Cities, Princes and Jinn from Arab Myths and Legends*. New York: Shocken Books, 1985, p. 14.

69. Quoted in Albert Hourani, *A History of the Arab Peoples*. Cambridge, MA: Harvard University Press, 1991, p. 52.

70. Quoted in Williams, *The Word of Islam*, p. 89.

Chapter 6: Islam's Medieval Empires

71. Durant, *The Age of Faith*, p. 202.

72. Quoted in John Alden Williams, ed., *Islam*. New York: Washington Square Press, 1961, p. 125.

73. Esposito, *Islam*, p. 59.

74. Hitti, *The Near East in History*, p. 308.

75. Quoted in Time-Life Books, eds., *Time Frame AD 1100–1200: The Divine Campaigns*. Alexandria, VA: Time-Life Books, 1988, p. 88.

76. Thomas J. Abercrombie, "The Sweep of Islam," in Grosvenor, *Great Religions of the World*, p. 243.

77. Stewart, *Early Islam*, pp. 163–164.

78. Quoted in *Time Frame AD 1100–1200*, p. 98.

79. Notes on this manuscript made by Gene R. Thursby, professor of religion, University of Florida, Gainesville, Florida, 1995.

80. Quoted in Larry Collins and Dominique Lapierre, *Freedom at Midnight*. New York: Simon and Schuster, 1975, p. 99.

81. McNeill, *The Rise of the West*, p. 619.

82. Hitti, *The Near East in History*, p. 378.

83. Hitti, *The Near East in History*, p. 381.

84. Esposito, *Islam*, p. 67.

Chapter 7: Imperial Islam in Decline

85. McNeill, *The Rise of the West*, p. 694.

86. Payne, *The History of Islam*, p. 284.

87. Hitti, *The Near East in History,* p. 431.

88. Quoted in Williams, *The Word of Islam*, p. 164.

89. McNeill, *The Rise of the West*, p. 695.

90. Quoted in Hourani, *A History of the Arab Peoples*, p. 272.

91. Quoted in Walter T. Wallbank, Alastair M. Taylor, and George Barr Carson Jr., *Civilization: Past and Present*, vol. 2. Chicago: Scott, Foresman and Company, 1965, p. 237.

92. Quoted in Esposito, *Islam*, p. 129.

93. Stewart, *Early Islam*, p. 170.

Chapter 8: Islam in Modern Times

94. Hourani, *A History of the Arab Peoples*, p. 264.

95. Quoted in Bernard Lewis, *Islam in History*. Chicago: Open Court Publishing, 1993, p. 222.

96. Quoted in Mansfield, *The New Arabians*, p. 51.

97. Thursby, notes.

98. Quoted in Collins and Lapierre, *Freedom at Midnight*, p. 331.

99. Hourani, *A History of the Arab Peoples*, p. 351.

100. Hourani, *A History of the Arab Peoples*, p. 351.

101. Bernard Lewis, "Islam and Liberal Democracy," *The Atlantic*, February 1993, p. 90.

102. Mansfield, *The New Arabians*, p. 165.

103. Lewis, "Islam and Liberal Democracy," p. 91.

104. William Pfaff, "Reflections: Islam and the West," the *New Yorker*, January 28, 1991, p. 88.

105. Armstrong, *Muhammad*, p. 180.

For Further Reading

Khairat Al-Saleh, *Fabled Cities, Princes and Jinn from Arab Myths and Legends.* New York: Shocken Books, 1985. A beautifully illustrated and very readable book on the legends, stories, and ancient myths and beliefs of the pre-Islamic Arabs.

George W. Beshore, *Science in Early Islamic Culture.* New York: Franklin Watts, 1988. Discusses the major scientific discoveries during Islam's golden age.

Leonard F. Hobley, *Moslems and Islam,* East Sussex, England: Wayland Publishers, 1979. A concise summary of the history and major beliefs of Islam.

Scholastic Update, "The Faces of Islam," October 22, 1993. This entire issue offers secondary-school students an array of interesting articles on many modern aspects of Islam.

Reeva S. Simon and Stephen Wasserstein, *The Middle East: History, Culture, Geography.* New York: Globe Book Company, 1987. A primer text for the general reader, this volume contains an informative section on Islam.

Desmond Stewart and the editors of Time-Life Books, *Early Islam.* New York: Time-Life Books, 1967. A cursory history of Islam, ranging from its origin to the late nineteenth century.

Sufism: The Alchemy of the Heart. San Francisco: Chronicle Books, 1993. A colorfully illustrated, compact book with thought-provoking passages of Sufi literature that explore the mystical side of Islam.

Richard Worth, *Israel and the Arab States.* New York: Franklin Watts, 1983. This brief but interesting book gives the background of the ongoing conflict between Israel and its Muslim neighbors.

Works Consulted

Karen Armstrong, *Muhammad: A Biography of the Prophet.* San Francisco: Harper San Francisco, 1992. A highly readable and informative book for both the scholar and the general reader meant to strip away many of the myths and prejudices that have developed in the West against Muhammad.

Steven Barboza, *American Jihad: Islam After Malcolm X.* New York: Doubleday, 1993. A fascinating mix of profiles of and interviews with a wide variety of American Muslims.

Ernle Bradford, *The Sundered Cross: The Story of the Fourth Crusade.* Englewood Cliffs, N.J.: Prentice-Hall, 1967. A detailed, scholarly account of a major crusade, enriched with primary sources.

Jacob Bronowski, *The Ascent of Man.* Boston: Little, Brown, 1973. A popular-science book written by a well-known scholar traces the development of science through the ages.

Joel Carmichael, *The Shaping of the Arabs.* New York: Macmillan, 1967. A scholarly yet highly readable account of Arabic history and Islamic civilization.

David Carroll and the editors of the Newsweek Book Division, *The Taj Mahal.* New York: Newsweek Book Division, 1972. A readable and colorfully illustrated history of the Taj Mahal for the general reader and scholar alike.

Larry Collins and Dominique Lapierre, *Freedom at Midnight.* New York: Simon and Schuster, 1975. A fascinating and page-turning history of the partition of India.

Will Durant, *The Age of Faith.* New York: Simon and Schuster, 1950. An entertaining and informative volume on medieval civilization, which provides analysis of Muhammad and early Islam.

John L. Esposito, *Islam: The Straight Path.* New York: Oxford University Press, 1991. An excellent academic resource on a wide range of aspects of Islam.

Grolier Classics, Omar Khayyám, *Rubáiyát of Omar Khayyám.* Danbury, CT: Grolier, 1956. An anthology of world literature classics.

Gilbert M. Grosvenor, ed., *Great Religions of the World.* Washington, DC: National Geographic Society, 1971. A highly illustrated, brief overview of the world's major religions.

Dilip Hiro, *Holy Wars: The Rise of Islamic Fundamentalism.* New York: Routledge, Chapman, and Hall, 1989. A readable account of the roots of Islam's fundamentalism movement.

Philip K. Hitti, *The Near East in History.* Princeton, NJ: Van Nostrand, 1961. A scholarly yet readable history of the Near East from the dawn of earliest civilizations to the late 1950s.

Albert Hourani, *A History of the Arab Peoples.* Cambridge, MA: Harvard University Press, 1991. A comprehensive, scholarly work.

Muhammad Zafrulla Khan, trans., *The Quran*. New York: Olive Branch Press, 1991. The Muslim holy book.

Bernard Lewis, *Islam in History*. Chicago: Open Court Publishing, 1993. A collection of essays on many aspects of Islam by a renowned scholar.

———, "Islam and Liberal Democracy," *The Atlantic*, February 1993. This article deals with abstract issues concerning Islam.

William H. McNeill, *The Rise of the West*. Chicago: University of Chicago Press, 1963. A scholarly work on the history of the world with an emphasis on how Western civilization rose to prominence in modern times.

Peter Mansfield, *The New Arabians*. Chicago: Ferguson Publishing, 1981. A work that explores the historical background of the modern Arabians.

Jean Mathe, *The Civilization of Islam*. Translated by David Macrae. New York: Crescent Books, 1980. An informative and illustrated work on the cultural aspects of Islamic society.

Robert Payne, *The History of Islam*. New York: Dorset Press, 1990. A remarkably readable history, filled with numerous colorful anecdotes and descriptions of Islam's movers and shakers.

Don Peretz, *The Middle East Today*, 3rd ed. New York: Holt, Rinehart and Winston, 1978. A thoroughly researched book with informative material on the rise of Islam.

William Pfaff, "Reflections: Islam and the West," *The New Yorker*, January 28, 1991. A magazine article summarizing the background for the unrest in the Middle East.

Readings in World History. Orlando, FL: Harcourt Brace Jovanovich, 1990. A compilation of primary sources.

George Seldes, *The Great Thoughts*. New York: Ballantine, 1985. A compilation of short passages on many of the greatest ideas in history.

Huston Smith, *The Religions of Man*. New York: Harper and Row, 1958. A readable and insightful study of humanity's spiritual quest.

Bertold Spuler, *History of the Mongols*. Translated by Helga Drummond and Stuart Drummond. New York: Dorset Press, 1968. A history based on a compilation of thirteenth- and fourteenth-century primary sources from both Eastern and Western sources.

Desmond Stewart, *Mecca*. New York: Newsweek Book Division, 1980. An interestingly written and beautifully illustrated book on the history of Islam's holiest city. For the general reader.

Desmond Stewart and the editors of Time-Life Books, *Early Islam*. New York: Time-Life Books, 1967. A cursory history of Islam, ranging from its origin to the late nineteenth century.

Time-Life Books, eds., *Time Frame AD 600–800: The March of Islam*. Alexandria, VA: Time-Life Books, 1988. A major section of this book provides a well-written though highly compressed account of the birth and rise of Islam.

———, *Time Frame AD 1100–1200: The Divine Campaigns*. Alexandria, VA:

Time-Life Books, 1988. This volume features well-written accounts of the Crusades and the Muslim takeover of India in the Middle Ages.

——, *Time Frame AD 1950–1990: The Nuclear Age*. Alexandria, VA: Time-Life Books, 1990. A concise overview of the emergence of modern-day Islam, with a special focus on its fundamentalist movement.

Walter T. Wallbank, Alastair M. Taylor, and George Barr Carson Jr., *Civilization: Past and Present*, vol 2. Chicago: Scott, Foresman and Company, 1965. An unusually readable college-level textbook.

H. G. Wells, *The Outline of History*. Garden City, NY: Garden City Publishing, 1920. A terse, popular history of humanity.

John Alden Williams, ed., *Islam*. New York: Washington Square Press, 1961. A compilation of writings from the Koran and other important Islamic sources.

——, *The Word of Islam*. Austin, TX: University of Texas Press, 1994. A scholarly work that uses original texts to emphasize the essentials of Islamic thought.

Index

Picture Credits

About the Author

John Dunn is a freelance writer and high school history teacher. He has taught in Georgia, Florida, North Carolina, and Germany. As a writer and journalist, he has published over 250 articles and stories in more than 20 periodicals, as well as scripts for audiovisual productions and a children's play. His book *The Russian Revolution* was published in 1993, and *The Relocation of the North American Indian* in 1994, both by Lucent Books. He lives with his wife and two daughters in Ocala, Florida.